Modern
New York

Modern New York

The Illustrated Story of Architecture in the Five Boroughs from 1920 to Today

Written and illustrated by
Lukas Novotny

RIZZOLI
NEW YORK

New York · Paris · London · Milan

Contents

Introduction

New York remains the ultimate big city in people's minds worldwide, even though by physical size it has long been overtaken by overseas giants. Its skyline, cultural richness, and global population made it into not only an ideal setting for romantic comedies but also an irresistible magnet for people who want to prove something—including the author of this book. While US immigration policy did not allow me to move permanently to the city, it didn't stop me from writing and illustrating this book.

Modern New York untangles the messy history of the last hundred years, which took the Big Apple on a wild roller coaster ride that swayed between the peaks of incredible prosperity and the downs of unimaginable disaster. This thrilling story is told through a selection of buildings that mixes famous landmarks and little-known local gems from across the five boroughs. And scattered throughout the book is the evolution of New York City's mass transit, which, perhaps like nowhere else, influenced its city's shape and form.

THE TITLE GUARANTEE COMPANY

Paramount

OPENING INAUGURATION PERFORMANCE
WORLD'S MOST MAGNIFICENT THEATER
BUILT FOR 4000 FPL GREAT THEATER

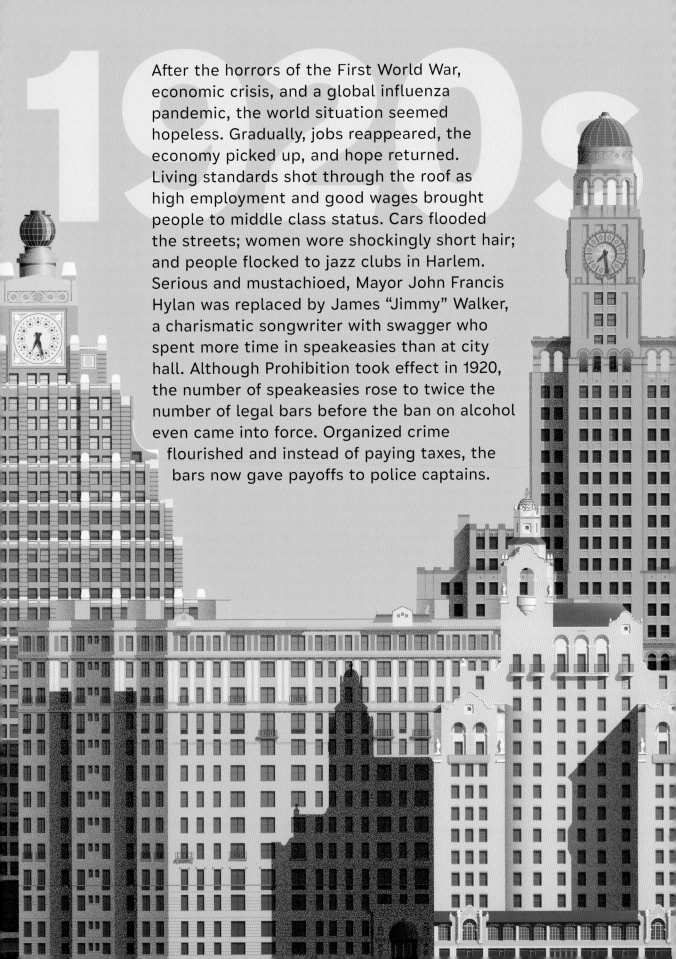

After the horrors of the First World War, economic crisis, and a global influenza pandemic, the world situation seemed hopeless. Gradually, jobs reappeared, the economy picked up, and hope returned. Living standards shot through the roof as high employment and good wages brought people to middle class status. Cars flooded the streets; women wore shockingly short hair; and people flocked to jazz clubs in Harlem. Serious and mustachioed, Mayor John Francis Hylan was replaced by James "Jimmy" Walker, a charismatic songwriter with swagger who spent more time in speakeasies than at city hall. Although Prohibition took effect in 1920, the number of speakeasies rose to twice the number of legal bars before the ban on alcohol even came into force. Organized crime flourished and instead of paying taxes, the bars now gave payoffs to police captains.

AMERICAN RADIATOR [1]
(Bryant Park Hotel)
Raymond Hood
40 W 40th St, Midtown
1924, Manhattan

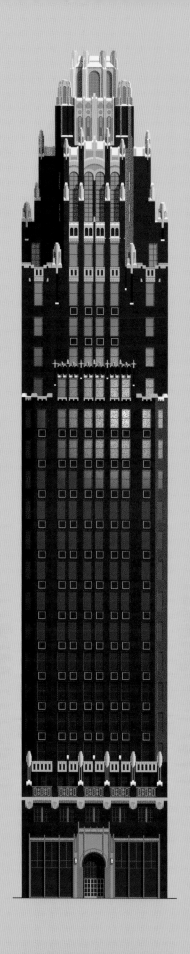

Raymond Hood didn't seem to have many prospects. Despite having graduated from prestigious architecture schools, he was unemployed, in debt, and over forty. One of his few commissions was a redesign of a speakeasy, for which he was paid in liquor. On the day his first child was born, he was fired from his job designing radiator covers for American Radiator. He was on the brink of giving up architecture, going back to his hometown of Pawtucket, Rhode Island, and getting a job at a local bank.[1]

Hood gave it one last shot, teaming up with John Mead Howells and sending a design to the *Chicago Tribune* architectural competition, one of the first truly international architectural contests. There were a total of 260 proposals from twenty-three countries. This proved to be a hugely important event, but only one design could win—and it was Hood and Howells's. The design received enormous attention, and almost overnight Hood became one of the most famous architects in the country.

After the success in Chicago, American Radiator (the company that had earlier fired Hood) asked him to design their headquarters, the **AMERICAN RADIATOR BUILDING [1]** (now the Bryant Park Hotel). He happily obliged and didn't hold back. Once built, its outlandish appearance stopped passersby in their tracks. From a row of sedate brown buildings dramatically rose a black tower decorated with golden detailing that shimmered in the sun. At night, the building was theatrically lit, the first skyscraper in the city to be.

Despite having designed some of the most visually impressive buildings in the United States, Hood didn't consider himself an artist. He pointed out that the times had changed and now modern architects collaborated with plumbers and engineers, rather than with painters and sculptors.

Hood could be surprisingly laid-back and gave his young assistants free rein, especially on Friday afternoons when he met up with architect mates like Ralph Walker and Joseph Urban for their "Four-Hour Lunch Club." Hard working and hard drinking, Hood had a career that lasted only twelve years before his early death, yet he managed to influence New York City's architecture like few before and after him.

Bizarrely, he later became an inspiration for a villain architect in Ayn Rand's 1943 book *The Fountainhead*. Rand saw Hood's ability to evolve his style with the times and the client's needs as a weakness and at odds with the strong individualism of people like Frank Lloyd Wright (on whom the book's hero is modeled). In the 1980s, people influenced by Rand's books—like Donald Trump—would gain influence over New York and later the whole country.

MACY'S THANKSGIVING DAY PARADE. The department store first organized its iconic Thanksgiving parade in 1924 with elephants, bears, and monkeys on loan from the Central Park Zoo. The unruly animals were replaced by slightly more controllable balloons three years later, which were then "released into the wild" at the parade's end. Macy's would offer cash to anyone who could hunt them down and return them to the store. Felix the Cat, the first character balloon, went out with a bang when it landed on electric wires and caught fire.[2]

A prominent Art Deco architect with a meteoric career, Walker was one of Hood's drinking buddies. Born in Waterbury, Connecticut, Walker was only thirty-four when he was put in charge of designing the **BARCLAY-VESEY BUILDING [2]** (also known as 100 Barclay/Verizon Building). It was built on a large, skewed-rectangle site, near busy Hudson wharves. The area's noise and smoke made it cheap, if not desirable. The building served as headquarters for the New York Telephone Company.

The immense size of the building's base—unusual before mechanical ventilation—made the deep interiors unusable as office space, but that wasn't a problem because the entire core was crowded with telephone switching equipment. The base rose eighteen floors up to a flat top, out of which a chunky square tower shot up all the way to the thirty-second floor. The building's creative massing and understated decoration won Walker much praise.

Walker was inspired by the design that placed second at the *Tribune* tower competition—similar to Hood's American Radiator Building—by Eero Saarinen, who had finally discovered a style suitable for skyscrapers, one that didn't wrap them in historicizing dress. Walker described his own building as "one that looks but little to the past, much to the present, and therefore tries to glimpse the future."

CHECKER H, 1923. Cab driving was a wild affair in the early 1920s, as drivers would get into fistfights for spots in popular locations. Because there was no regulation on the maximum number of cars, competition was tense and driving was dangerous.[3] In 1929, there were more than one thousand traffic deaths—mostly pedestrians hit by drivers—about five times as many as today.[4]

BARCLAY-VESEY BUILDING [2]
(Verizon Building, 100 Barclay)
Ralph Walker
140 West Street, Financial District
1927, Manhattan

In the Theater District around Times Square, many didn't like this glimpse of the future. The movie industry took its first steps in New York but departed for California for better weather and its distance from patents on filming equipment. Later, it returned with a vengeance. In a short time, the business exploded, and in 1928 there were an incredible 548 movie palaces in New York City alone, double the number of spoken-drama theaters.[5]

Film studios would not only produce movies, but also distribute them through a network of their own cinemas. Paramount Studios set up a beachhead right in the heart of Manhattan at Times Square with its **PARAMOUNT BUILDING [3]**. The 3,664-seat cinema premiered the biggest blockbusters of the day, including international hits like *Metropolis* (1927). The building was designed by experienced Chicago architecture firm Rapp & Rapp, who had hundreds of other cinema designs under its belt. The theater opened in 1926 with the silent film *God Gave Me Twenty Cents*; the first talkie would come a year later.

The building was supposedly set to resemble the mountain in the studio's logo. The pile was crowned by an illuminated globe. (One critic speculated it was actually an incinerator for the ashes of departed films.) The globe had to be painted black during the Second World War to maintain blackout conditions to help keep the harbor safe from Nazi submarines.

SAVOIA-MARCHETTI S-56 NYPD FLYING BOAT. A special NYPD unit was established to clip the wings of show-off pilots that dangerously buzzed the city in what was called "rouge aviation." This was before pilot licenses and ground control became a thing. Reckless and incompetent flyers caused eight deaths and twenty-one injuries when showing off.[6]

But there were other modes of entertainment apart from going to the movies. Coney Island in Brooklyn was a popular spot filled with amusement parks (also appearing in many early films). It was also a place of historic importance: the first American hot dog was sold there, albeit called a "dachshund sandwich." One of the less notable attractions was the miniature town of Lilliputia, where three hundred little people lived in an experimental community that was complete with its own fire station and parliament. The Wonder Wheel and Cyclone, attractions that entertain to this day, were also both opened during the 1920s.

HALF MOON HOTEL [4] was built nearby for a more high-brow clientele in hopes of making Coney Island a renowned summer resort. The large 400-room hotel was designed in a flamboyant Spanish Colonial style. But what made it famous wasn't the architecture, rather it was one of its visitors: Abe "Kid Twist" Reles. A career gangster, Reles cut a deal with the police to avoid the electric chair, testifying against his pals in Murder Inc., a criminal organization of Jewish and Italian mobsters responsible for hundreds of murders.

HALF MOON HOTEL [4]
George B. Post and Sons
Boardwalk at West 29th
St, Coney Island
1927-1996, Brooklyn

Once Reles turned informant, he was kept hidden under constant police protection in the Half Moon Hotel. However, despite being guarded by five detectives, Reles mysteriously "fell" out of a window on the night before his testimony. Newspapers had a field day with sensational front-page headlines like "The Canary Who Could Sing But Not Fly."

Meanwhile, on the other side of Brooklyn, **WILLIAMSBURGH SAVINGS BANK TOWER [5]** (now One Hanson Place) sprouted. The tower's banking room was one of the most stunning interiors in the whole city: it was sized like a church hall, with a high arched ceiling and huge tinted-glass windows. Built near Long Island Terminal and the intersection of Atlantic and Flatbush Avenues, it was seen as the first step of the borough's new business district. Little did anyone know that the tower would remain the tallest skyscraper in Brooklyn for the next eighty years.

But the economy was still booming, and land prices were skyrocketing, requiring buildings to be built higher and faster to pay for the land. This mad pace, seen on building sites all over New York City, claimed victims. Construction deaths shot up by 61 percent from 1927 to when the Tower opened in 1929. By then, the building industry had become the deadliest in the state, second only to mining.

Brooklyn was becoming the most populous borough in the mid-1920s, as it offered close proximity to the city for people pushed out of Manhattan by growing commerce and industry. Commuting to work in Manhattan while living in the outer boroughs became possible thanks to rising wages and the expanding network of trains, subways, and streetcars.

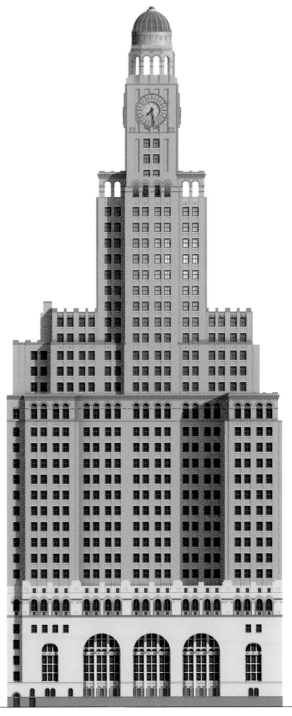

WILLIAMSBURGH SAVINGS BANK TOWER [5] *(One Hanson Place)*
Halsey, McCormack and Helmer
1 Hanson Place, Fort Greene
1929, Brooklyn

New lines also lead to the Bronx, which was the fastest-growing borough in New York City. In a single decade it absorbed half a million new residents, many of whom were Jews moving from the tenements of the Lower East Side. Grand Concourse, a boulevard modeled on the Champs-Élysées in Paris, stretched five miles from near Yankee Stadium. Opened in 1923, Yankee Stadium was the largest ballpark in the country. Grand Concourse was a magnet for new construction, and living there was the dream of many an ambitious Jewish family.

1749 Grand Concourse, better known as the **LEWIS MORRIS APARTMENTS [6]**, became the most reputable address on the boulevard. At eleven stories, the building towered over its surroundings and provided views of the Manhattan skyline from its apartments. The entrance had a white-gloved doorman, and the pink marble lobby contained fountains. The block was filled with the most high-tech amenities of the day, such as a telephone in every apartment and mail chute on every floor.

The building's prestige was further cemented when it somehow became home to a variety of doctors who had set up shop on the lower floors. Nearly the whole neighborhood would go there for dental work. As the area continued to prosper, local builders, inspired by Art Deco structures rising in Manhattan, built dozens of handsome jazzy apartment blocks that would define the boulevard in the 1930s.

LEWIS MORRIS APARTMENTS [6]
Edward Raldiris
1749 Grand Concourse, Mount Hope
1923, the Bronx

The decade brought changes for African Americans too. More Black policemen and doctors were hired, and overall employment was high. Harlem became the largest urban Black community in the country, its population doubling in ten years as it became a destination for poor families from the rural South. Knowing that Black families had little chance of finding housing outside of Harlem, disreputable landlords charged outrageous rents. The neighborhood's poverty and substandard housing led to illness and mortality rates that were 40 percent higher than in the rest of the city.

Enter John D. Rockefeller, Jr., son of the richest American of all time. His father had gained the world's monopoly on oil refinement not only through business genius, but also the ruthless destruction of his competitors, which made him one of the most hated men in the country. Junior, as he was known, wanted to change that and hired Ivy Lee, one of the earliest pioneers in the field of public relations, to clean up the family image. The advice was simple: start using (some) of the money for good causes.

Following Lee's advice, Junior built the **DUNBAR APARTMENTS [7]** in Harlem—the first quality development for African Americans in the country. He also bankrolled Dunbar National Bank, based in the building, which was the first bank under Black management. The unusual development was designed by unusual character Andrew J. Thomas. Orphaned at age thirteen, Thomas worked as a rent collector for a realtor speculator and had witnessed firsthand the awful conditions in which people were living. Working as a timekeeper at construction sites, Thomas taught himself drawing and technical knowledge in the evenings and became an architect.

DUNBAR APARTMENTS [7]
Andrew J. Thomas
226 W 150th St, Harlem
1926, Manhattan

**NEW YORK CENTRAL
BUILDING [8]**
(Helmsley Building)
Warren and Wetmore
230 Park Ave, Midtown
1929, Manhattan

Meanwhile Midtown continued to prosper, stealing the thunder from Lower Manhattan, the original economic heart of Gotham from the start of the fur trade with Native Americans. There was even "new" land available in Midtown: electrification of trains meant that the vast Grand Central railyard could be built over, which was previously impossible because of smoke-churning locomotives. A new crop of hotels and office buildings quickly grew over it.

One of the last free spots was taken by the **NEW YORK CENTRAL BUILDING [8]** (Helmsley Building, today), built for the railroad company of the same name. The building's foundations were steel columns that stood between the dense network of tracks. They were wrapped in compressed cork to insulate them from the vibrations from the seven hundred trains screeching past each day. The building sophisticatedly linked itself into the complicated urban fabric of the area. The four portals allowed Park Avenue to pass through, including pedestrians who could use its link to the subway and the underground concourse of Grand Central.

Out of the wings that filled the site, right on the axis of Park Avenue, rose a thirty-five-story tower with a pyramidal roof. It didn't block the vista, but rather enhanced it; the tower's unconventional silhouette stood like an exclamation mark visible from fifty blocks away. But the undoing of the railroad—the automobile—was already in the making. The automobile revolutionized American life and began to hurt the railways' bottom line.

TRAFFIC TOWER. America was being redrawn by mass car ownership, and New York City was at the center of it. Between 1918 and 1931, the number of cars in the city increased sixfold.[7] Traffic was so slow a writer commented "any old fat lady will walk six blocks while a vehicle passes two."[8] In attempt to alleviate the problem, John A. Harriss, a former deputy police commissioner and a millionaire, introduced man-operated traffic towers on Fifth Avenue. He paid for their construction out of his own pocket.[9]

While most boroughs had relatively easy access to public transport linking them with "the city" (Manhattan), Staten Island was an exception. It was (and still is) the city's most-isolated and least-populated borough. It had been consolidated into Greater New York thirty years earlier. The union brought some benefits to the borough, such as new roads and improved services but also some points of contention that would never dissipate. On paper, Staten Island was part of the city, but it was only connected by ferry service.

Since New Jersey was much closer, it was not surprising that the first physical link to the mainland were the two new bridges that opened in 1928. One, the **OUTERBRIDGE CROSSING [9]**, was after the conveniently named first chairman of the Port Authority, Eugenius Harvey Outerbridge. The Port Authority, a joint agency run both by New Jersey and New York, was established to develop and run complex infrastructure in the 25-mile radius of the Statue of Liberty. The other span connecting New Jersey with Staten Island was the Goethals Bridge.

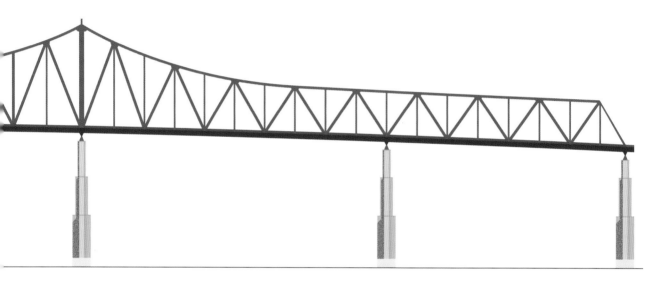

OUTERBRIDGE CROSSING [9]
J.A.L. Waddell
NY 440, Charleston
1928, Staten Island

TUGBOATS. New York Harbor was the busiest and the most important in the country. Keeping the port running were hundreds of tugboats, many of which became diesel-powered in the 1920s. But some steam-powered tugs kept pushing on until the 1960s.

While most of Staten Island remained rural, commercial access was improved by the new bridges and that helped manufacturing to flourish. The new jobs in turn attracted new residents. Queens, another sleepy borough, also prospered. Its population skyrocketed 60 percent from 1910 to 1927. It was these population explosions in the outer boroughs that pushed New York City to become the biggest city in the world, even beating out London.

Businesses dealing with real estate had so much work lined up that they had to expand fast. The **SUFFOLK TITLE AND GUARANTEE COMPANY BUILDING [10]**, new offices for a company insuring loans and mortgages, was built in Jamaica, which was still a very suburban-looking part of Queens with detached houses and tree-lined streets.

Designed by the duo of Dennison and Hirons, one from New Jersey, one from Manhattan, the building brought the best of Art Deco to town, and with it gorgeously detailed ornamental metalwork surrounding the entrance as well as colorful glazed terra-cotta panels. The decoration was the work of renowned sculptor Rene Chembellan, who had also worked on the Williamsburgh Savings Bank Tower.

SUFFOLK TITLE AND GUARANTEE COMPANY BUILDING [10]
Dennison & Hirons
90-04 161 St, Jamaica
1929, Queens

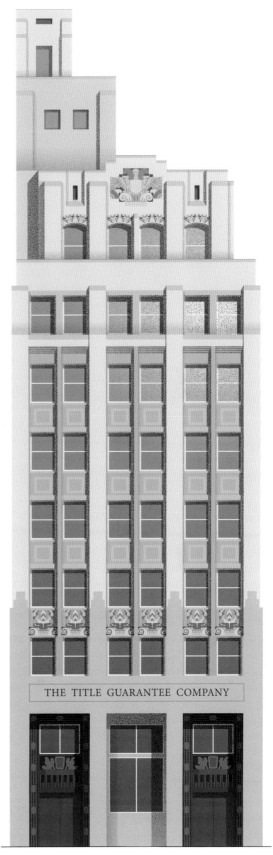

THE TITLE GUARANTEE COMPANY

NEW YORK MUNICIPAL
AIRPORT

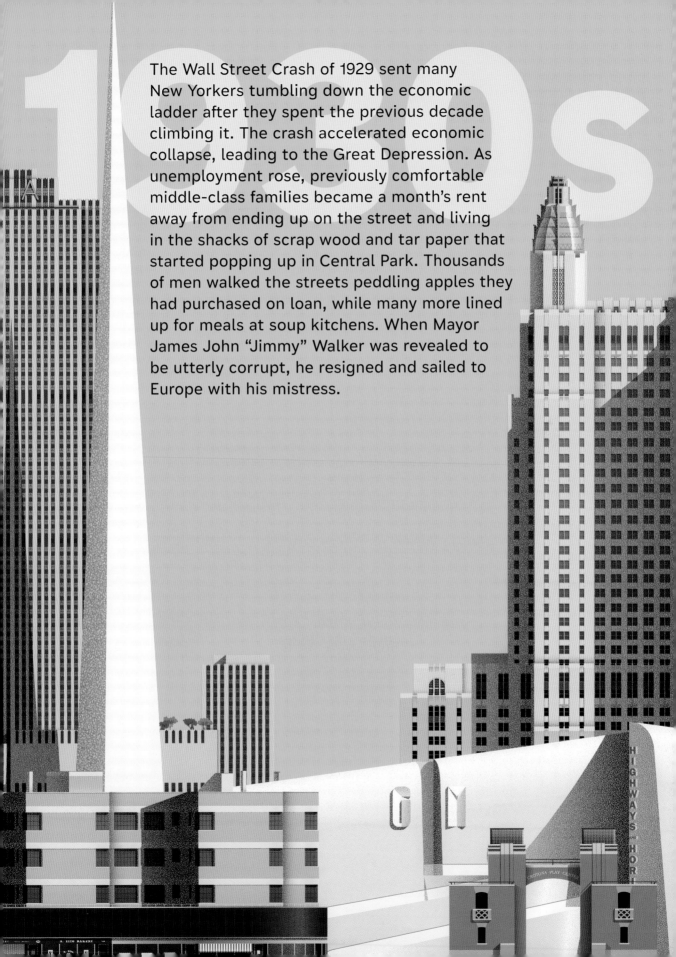

The Wall Street Crash of 1929 sent many New Yorkers tumbling down the economic ladder after they spent the previous decade climbing it. The crash accelerated economic collapse, leading to the Great Depression. As unemployment rose, previously comfortable middle-class families became a month's rent away from ending up on the street and living in the shacks of scrap wood and tar paper that started popping up in Central Park. Thousands of men walked the streets peddling apples they had purchased on loan, while many more lined up for meals at soup kitchens. When Mayor James John "Jimmy" Walker was revealed to be utterly corrupt, he resigned and sailed to Europe with his mistress.

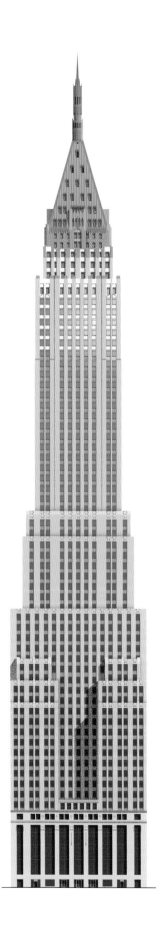

The economic cooldown led to the cancellation of most planned construction projects across the city. Still, some buildings rose, perhaps in an attempt to outpace the speed at which money melted away from their investors' pockets. The public, starved of positive news in those grim times, clung on those few projects as happy distractions, seeing them as signs that everything wasn't over yet. In the avalanche of bad news, the war that waged between three Manhattan skyscrapers battling it out for the title of tallest building in the world was a welcomed break. The press dubbed this contest a "Race to the Sky," and it was the last extravagance of the Roaring Twenties.

The speed at which **40 WALL STREET [11]** (now the Trump Building, Bank of Manhattan) raced to completion was breathtaking. One day, clerks working in the headquarters of the Manhattan Company noticed their coffee cups shaking because builders had begun to dig foundations for the new skyscraper right in their basement. A couple of weeks later, when the old offices were finally vacated, 1,200 workers swarmed the site. Demolition and foundation crews worked side by side in a synchronized effort, in three shifts, seven days a week.

Responsible for the building's plans was architect H. Craig Severance. Charismatic and wealthy, Severance moved comfortably through New York's highest circles and collected their design commissions with ease. Severance usually focused on grooming the clients and delegated the "small matters," such as actual design work, to others. He found a perfect partner in William Van Alen, whose creative talent supplemented Severance's business skills. But after thirteen years, their union turned sour, and a bitter separation followed. Now alone, Severance still had no shortage of clients, but he struggled to keep as high a design standard as before.

40 WALL STREET [11]
(Trump Building,
Bank of Manhattan)
H. Craig Severance, Yasuo Matsui
40 Wall St, Financial District
1929, Manhattan

Severance's most recent building had received such a poor review in the *New Yorker* that he sued them for damages. 40 Wall Street, the world's tallest building, was to re-establish his prestige.

There was just one problem: the **CHRYSLER BUILDING [12]**, already under construction in Midtown, had the same ambition. What's more, it had been designed by his former partner, William Van Alen. The rapid construction of Severance's skyscraper meant that they actually caught up with that of the Chrysler Building, which had started months before. Severance delegated the design work to Japanese-born Yasuo Matsui, ordering additional floors and a steeply pitched roof to be sure the title of the world's tallest building would be theirs.

After the final topping of 40 Wall Street, Severance celebrated, sure of his victory. No one was now paying much attention to Van Alen's Chrysler Building, which was practically finished. Automobile magnate Walter Chrysler, its owner, used to run Buick, owned by General Motors (GM). After several years of collecting an astronomically high salary he left the company over a disagreement with his bosses at GM. He would eventually rival them with his very own company.

Chrysler decided to plant his new headquarters in New York City, America's financial and cultural center. Also, New York wasn't Detroit, considered the traditional "car capital," which he hated. The building was not only going to be the company headquarters but a statement about the man himself. Making it the world's tallest building seemed only natural to Chrysler, who had been named "Man of the Year" by *Time* magazine in 1928. He paid for the building out of his own pocket.

CHRYSLER BUILDING [12]
William Van Alen
405 Lexington Ave, Midtown
1930, Manhattan

EMPIRE STATE BUILDING [13]
Shreve, Lamb and Harmon
350 Fifth Ave, Midtown
1931, Manhattan

No expense was spared on the elaborate brick facade adorned by huge gargoyles in the shape of the Chrysler car hood ornament or the majestic lobby and car showroom at ground level. The building's glamorous crown was clad in Nirosta steel, a special type of stainless alloy. The steel had been tested in the carmaker's laboratories to ensure it would keep its silver-like quality in New York's smog and weather.

During construction, the plans were repeatedly amended to keep up with the height of the rapidly rising 40 Wall Street. Then came a bombshell. The news of the planned **EMPIRE STATE BUILDING [13]** got out. This mammoth of a building was to be far taller than both the competing towers. To add insult to injury, it was financed by Chrysler's old enemy, John J. Raskob from GM. Now it was personal for both Chrysler and his architect.

Livid, Chrysler gave Van Alen a blank check and told him to do whatever he needed to do to beat the competition. The architect happily obliged. His solution was to extend the crown and add a little surprise on top. In a now legendary move, a tall spire was secretly assembled inside the building's elevator shaft. Once the 122-foot spike was hoisted up, the Chrysler Building became tall enough to beat both the just-completed 40 Wall Street and the planned Empire State. In short, it was now the tallest building in the world!

Van Alen didn't celebrate for long. An architect first and businessman second, he forgot to sign a contract with Chrysler at the start of the project—a mistake many freelancers know only too well. Demanding the standard fee (6 percent of the building cost) from Chrysler, Van Alen was rebuffed and had to sue him. Although he eventually won the fee in court, his reputation was in tatters as one simply did not sue the "Man of the Year." Van Alen spent the rest of his days teaching sculpture.

Raskob, the developer of the Empire State Building, didn't really care for Chrysler. Construction of the tallest building in the world wasn't driven by his ego but was simply an investment. During the twenties he accumulated such wealth that all ten of his children would have a hard time trying to spend it all. Raskob was a financial executive at GM, where he had pioneered installment payments for purchasing cars, a novelty at the time. Just eight years later, 60 percent of customers were buying their cars this way. Alongside other super-rich at the time, Raskob was able to manipulate the stock market to reap huge profits. Ironically, two months before the 1929 crash, Raskob wrote that, "Everybody ought to be rich," and encouraged ordinary people to invest in the ever-rising stock market.

When the economic bubble burst, the Empire State Building was—unlike 40 Wall Street and the Chrysler Building—still only a plan on paper. It would have been reasonable to postpone the project. The property market was clearly oversaturated, and toward the end of the decade landlords were struggling to fill office space. Raskob pushed on.

KING KONG, 1933. The observation deck on top of the Empire State Building became so popular that in the first year it brought as much profit as all the rents from the entire building. The giant, love-struck gorilla from King Kong (1933) obviously went up for free.

The high cost of the land, the previous site of the famous **WALDORF-ASTORIA HOTEL [14]**, increased the need for a tight budget. For example, the 6,500 windows used were standard off-the-shelf models and were kept in original anti-rust tomato red. The construction process was streamlined into a symphony of movements. Every day, hundreds of trucks delivered material to the site in a perfect rhythm, never waiting for more than a couple of minutes to unload. Steel arrived from mills in Pittsburgh just hours after it was made and was still warm to the touch. Dancing in the sky without any safety equipment were some 3,500 workers.

After the stunt of erecting the secret spire, the Chrysler Building's height had surpassed the original design for the Empire State Building. In response, the architects added floors to increase the height. Still, they remained fearful. They wondered if Van Alen had hidden another rod inside of the infamous spire that could be released upward at the last minute. To be sure, they decided to install a spire of their own. The original idea was that it would be a mooring mast for airships. The fragile, gas-filled machines the size of ocean liners were supposed to anchor there and allow passengers to board—all while the winds raged at 1,250 feet.

It obviously couldn't work, but it caught people's imagination and that was enough. The planned baggage rooms and customs for the international travelers inside the mooring mast were quietly transformed into the world's highest soda fountain. The Depression had made everything cheaper, so the building was finished weeks before the deadline and under budget.

On the evening of the grand opening, President Herbert Hoover pressed a golden telegraph key in the Oval Office that illuminated lights on the skyscraper. Now it was time for tenants to move in, though there weren't many. The realtors managed to attract the Model Brassiere Company, a large manufacturer of corsets and bras, but that wasn't enough to support the building. With a mere 25 percent occupancy, the skyscraper was soon rechristened the "Empty" State Building.

The building struggled, and it wasn't until 1946 that it was fully occupied, with some 15,000 workers. The rise of the Empire State Building exemplified the process seen on many Manhattan blocks—the vicious cycle of destruction and creation. The unfortunate building that had to make space for the new king of the hill was the Waldorf-Astoria Hotel, once called the "Unofficial Palace of New York." The establishment came into existence when two feuding cousins each built a hotel literally next door to each other. They were persuaded to put their bickering aside and join the hotels with a corridor for the sake of profit, if not family unity. The hotel's elaborate ballrooms quickly became the living room for the city's upper classes.

But New York City changes. And fast. Only twenty years after the hotel was built, it was deemed too old and in the wrong part of town. In Europe, a building of such status would have been treasured as a protected landmark to this day, but in New York it was dismembered and its remains were unceremoniously dumped into the sea. The resurrection of the Waldorf-Astoria Hotel took place between fashionable Lexington and Park Avenues, across the street from the New York Central Building. The site was strategically located near Grand Central Terminal and close to a growing variety of luxury stores, which slowly took over Fifth Avenue after the upper crust drifted north to new apartment houses facing Central Park.

WALDORF-ASTORIA HOTEL [14]
Schultze & Weaver
301 Park Ave, Midtown
1931, Manhattan

Schultze & Weaver, the architects, had had experience building large hotels everywhere from Florida to California, but nothing could have prepared them for this. Though they had a whole block, they had the challenging task to fit a luxury hotel, an apartment house, ballrooms, exhibition rooms, and garages into it. And it all had to balance on stilts wedged between rail tracks, which severely limited the basement, the usual place for the hotel services. One of the underground rail tracks was utilized as the hotel's own platform where travelers were unloaded directly from their private train cars into elevators that took them into the hotel upstairs.

With two thousand rooms, it became the largest hotel in the world once it opened. In the two towers, which also made it the tallest hotel in the world, were three hundred luxury residential suites, each having its own lobby, living room, dining room, and three to four bedrooms. In its new location, the Waldorf-Astoria Hotel quickly regained its reputation and became the place to stay for society's elite.

One industry, however, resisted the wooing of Midtown and remained loyal to Lower Manhattan: The Financial District. Banks didn't need to move closer to commerce; all they really wanted was proximity to other banks and downtown already had them. A group of bankers and lawyers working around Wall Street funded the **DOWNTOWN ATHLETIC CLUB [15]**. They wanted to have all the luxuries of a country club, but because of Manhattan land prices they could only afford a small plot—no bigger than a parking lot of a typical country club. But this was the golden age of a skyscraper, anything could fit, it just needed to be stacked vertically.

Billiard and card rooms were on one floor, bowling alleys on another, and squash courts on the next. The seventh floor was an English landscape golf course, complete with grassy hills, trees, and even a river. If this tiny, fake waterway wasn't enough, the whole twelfth floor was taken up by a big swimming pool. Wrestling and boxing were on the ninth, along with an oyster bar.

However, the strangest floor was the tenth. There, members had an artificial sunbath where they could catch the rays denied to them in the dark alleys of Lower Manhattan. Members had their muscles tended by masseurs in Turkish baths, and a special clinic provided colonic irrigation to flush out their systems. Once refreshed, men went to have a haircut and a clean shave from the barber on the same level.

After the first twelve floors of activities, the next five—containing dining rooms, kitchens, and lounges—were designed for socializing. Finally, the seventeenth floor was where the men were ready to meet women on the dance floor. Above this party room floor were twenty floors of small bedrooms that were advertised as "ideal for men who are free of family cares." Le Corbusier, one of the fathers of modern architecture, once said that "a house is a machine for living." Well, this "house" was a machine for self-indulgence.

GOODYEAR BLIMP, COLUMBIA. The silver blimp was used to test the possibility of mooring at the Empire State Building mast. The blimp arrived dangling a bundle of newspapers from a long rope and tried to deliver it to the mooring mast. On a third pass, a man leaned dangerously over the parapet, got the bundle, and quickly cut it off the rope. No more trials were made.[10]

**DOWNTOWN ATHLETIC CLUB
[15]** *(Downtown Club)*
Starrett & van Vleck
20 West St, Financial District
1931, Manhattan

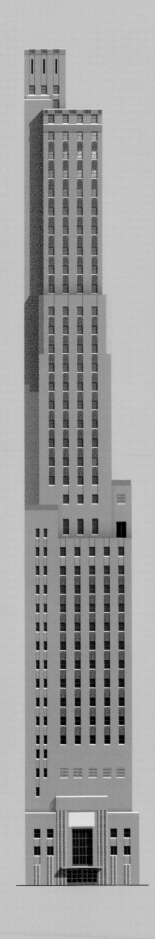

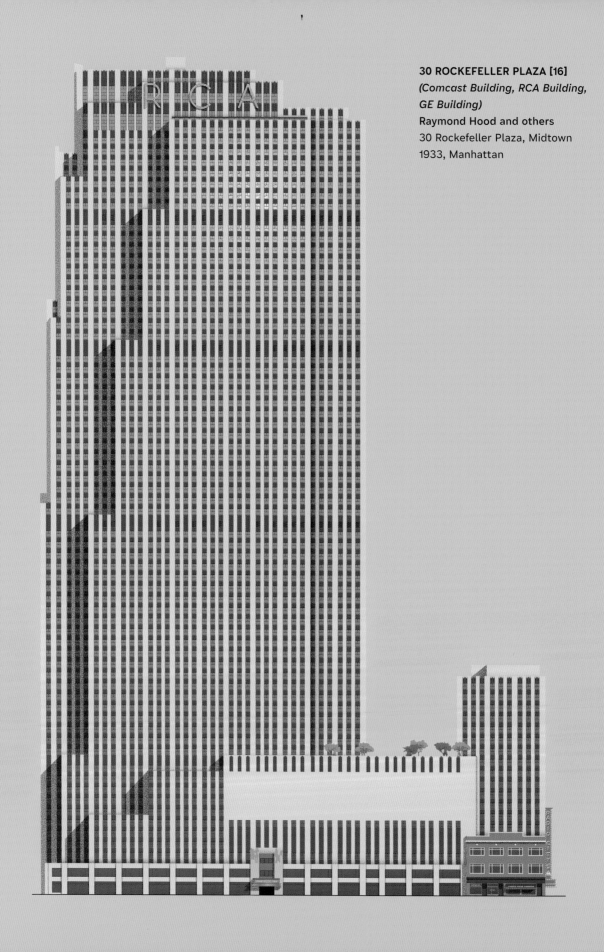

30 ROCKEFELLER PLAZA [16]
(Comcast Building, RCA Building, GE Building)
Raymond Hood and others
30 Rockefeller Plaza, Midtown
1933, Manhattan

After the Dunbar Apartments, John D. Rockefeller, Jr. continued in his wide-ranging philanthropic activities. He supported the Tuskegee Institute in Alabama, repairs of Versailles in France, and preservation of artifacts in Palestine. Closer to home, Rockefeller funded many New York City charities and was seen as an ideal sponsor of The New York Metropolitan Opera's plans to build a new hall. Junior agreed and leased three rundown blocks in Midtown from Columbia University for what was to be called the Metropolitan Square development.

WISDOM AT 30 ROCKEFELLER MAIN ENTRANCE. This signature piece was by Lee Lawrie, the nation's foremost architectural sculptor. Although John D. Rockefeller, Jr. generally gave the artists free rein, he was very involved with this piece because he despised the decoration above the building's north and south entrances and wanted to have at least one doorway he could use.[11]

The planned opera house was to be surrounded by commercial buildings, which would offset the construction cost. But the Depression brought a perfect storm. The Opera ran out of money and was dropped from the plans; the demand for commercial space disappeared; and Junior's net worth dropped by half. Nevertheless, he had already signed the lease and could not back out. The collection of rundown buildings, many of them brothels and speakeasies, earned only a fraction of his lease payments. He simply had to build.

Heading the project was John R. Todd, a dictatorial developer who had made his fortune in Manhattan real estate and saw architects only as a necessary evil. He is credited with statements like "for an architect, you have almost human intelligence." But few would complain about this as now six out of seven architects in the United States were unemployed, and this was one of very few projects still going.

The scale of Rockefeller Center was too large for a single architect, so a team was put together. Leading it was Hood, architect of the American Radiator Building, whose refusal to limit himself by architecture theories sat well with Todd. Together with Junior, this trio influenced the program and look of the Rockefeller Center. One of the youngest on the team was Wallace Harrison, who was related to the Rockefellers through marriage. He would later head construction of the United Nations Headquarters [32] and also unfairly claim credit for single-handedly designing Rockefeller Center.

The gap in the heart of the development left by the lost opera house was filled by the grandiose **30 ROCKEFELLER PLAZA [16]** (also known as the Comcast Building, RCA Building, GE Building). The building was home to the radio giant RCA, predecessor of today's big-tech companies. Predicting the bright future of the still nascent television broadcasting, large studios were built for its subsidiary NBC. To limit the noise and vibrations from the outside, the studios were built as a room-within-a-room standing on giant steel springs.

Since 1975, *Saturday Night Live* has broadcast live from the studios every weekend. (However, while Tina Fey's comedy *30 Rock* was supposedly set there, the show was actually filmed at Silvercup Studios in Queens.)

Another important piece of Rockefeller Center was Radio City Music Hall, the 6,000-seat vaudeville theater. It was designed with the help of S.L. Rothafel, known affectionately as "Roxy" after the theater he had built. Rothafel was a forward-looking showbiz mastermind and megalomaniac who usually brought great success to any entertainment palace. But that was not the case with Radio City. The much-anticipated opening night was a complete six-hour-long catastrophe. (Roxy must have wished his lawyers hadn't blocked his idea for pumping laughing gas into the theater.) He was eventually fired and the Music Hall was converted to the world's biggest cinema. It showed a fifty-minute live stage show before each screening, which included Roxy's brainchild, a group of young dancers called The Rockettes, and proved very popular.

The original idea behind Rockefeller Center might have started as a philanthropic act, but its purpose was to turn a profit. Junior's team went as far as successfully lobbying for a change to the state law that provided all theater employees with a day off each week. The amendment to the law took this benefit away from people working in "places combining film and live shows," in other words, Radio City. The dancers now performed in shows four times a day, seven days a week. Still, the Great Depression gave anyone with a paying job little to complain about. Up on the roof gardens, some were working even without pay—a bunch of chipmunks was released there to keep the excess roots and beetles at bay.

However, these savings were peanuts compared to money lost from the empty offices. Manhattan simply had too much vacant office space at a time when prospective tenants were bankrupt or downsizing. For example, 40 Wall Street had defaulted and was offered for a sale price lower than the cost of its elevators five years prior. To fill the offices, the Rockefellers asked suppliers, who were desperate for a gig at the virtually only construction project in the city, to move their business to the Center. And many of them did.

The new public space the Rockefeller Center provided became busy with workers on lunch breaks, shoppers, cinema-goers, and pedestrians using it as a shortcut between streets. Five men had full-time employment removing chewing gum and three others targeted cigarette butts. The Center succeeded not only economically, but it also became enmeshed in the fabric of Manhattan and was a model for other large-scale developments all over the world. Later, similarly scaled projects like Lincoln Center or the new Hudson Yards would fall far short of that.

THE AMBASSADOR ARMS [17]
Lucien Pisciotta
30 Daniel Low Terrace, St George
1932, Staten Island

Modern architecture trends were now spreading to the more underdeveloped borough of Staten Island. One of the few urbanized areas at the time was St. George, home of the ferry terminal and the only direct connection with Manhattan. But when work began on a subway tunnel under the Narrows tidal strait that was to link Brooklyn's Bay Ridge and Staten's Tompkinsville, expectations drove a building boom that replaced many of the small homes with large multi-family duplexes. Even apartment buildings started to appear.

One of them was the **AMBASSADOR ARMS [17]**, just a ten-minute walk from the ferry terminal. Set amongst suburban homes, the building dwarfed the surrounding homes and its Jazz Age facade was comparatively loud against the neighborhood's conservative houses. The exterior white brick was rhythmically interrupted by black strips as fashion dictated, but it was the main entrance that stole the show, with its stunning tile ornament in brilliant glazed colors. In later years, the magical quality of the building—and convenient commute to Manhattan—attracted people like Paul Newman and Martin Sheen, who lived there before their acting careers took off.

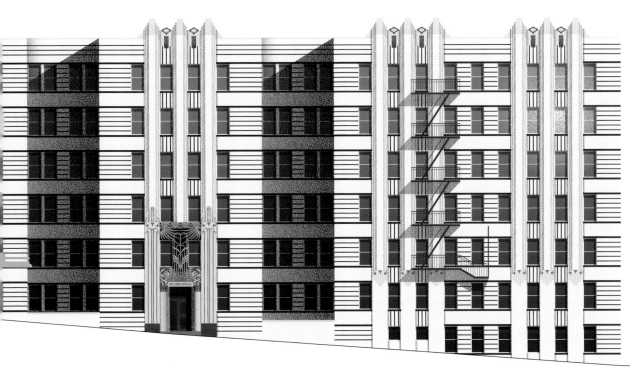

By the time the Ambassador Arms was finished in 1932, the boom was over. Digging on the subway link to Staten Island was halted due to funding issues, the Depression having sealed its fate. Unemployment began to reach record highs. Under President Franklin Delano Roosevelt, the government launched the Works Progress Administration (WPA) as a part of the New Deal. The WPA funded public projects that hired the masses of unemployed to build them. This new source of money and labor was skillfully tapped into by Robert Moses, the head of the city's Parks Department. Moses was also head of the Triborough Bridge and Tunnel Authority.

Moses held more power in New York City than most elected politicians. With his detailed knowledge of state law and political insight, he was able to gradually gather control and influence over construction of pretty much everything in the city. His genius of finding legal loopholes, drafting new bills, and manipulating the press helped him to cement his position as a "Master Builder" for three incredible decades.

Moses began working on great improvements to the city's parks and infrastructure and brought more federal money to the city than anyone else could. He built new beaches and connected them to the city by new parkways—roads surrounded by landscaped scenery. He created dozens of new parks and playgrounds and restored existing ones. An avid swimmer and believer in active relaxation, Moses built eleven new swimming pools across the city.

Manhattan and Brooklyn each got four pools, while the remaining boroughs had to make do with one apiece. The Bronx had **CROTONA PARK POOL [18]** in its eponymous park. As with the other pools, it was located in a mostly working-class area. Because the project was being built with WPA money, it had to use the cheapest materials—red brick and concrete. Regardless, Moses's team of architects designed stunning structures.

After paying an entrance fee, visitors were given a clean towel and a place to store their clothes. Before entering the pool area, everyone had to take a shower and walk through a shallow basin that disinfected their feet. Cleanliness was essential, and the pools set a new standard. Many of the swimmers lived in cold-water apartments and the hot shower would have been most welcomed. Even the pool itself could be heated if necessary, and in winter the generously sized bathhouse could be converted into a gymnasium.

Moses opened the pools gradually, one per week, to maximize publicity and to make politicians grateful for photo opportunities. Mayor Fiorello La Guardia was present, of course, to take credit as well. Born in Greenwich Village, La Guardia is deservedly considered the best mayor the city ever had.

Before being elected, La Guardia had an exciting career and saw the world. He could speak several languages—Italian, German, Hungarian, Croatian, Yiddish— and worked at Ellis Island for a time as a translator for newly arrived immigrants. Short and stocky, La Guardia was often seen racing to the scenes of fires in a motorcycle sidecar. He seemed to be everywhere, and a joke made the rounds that there wasn't one mayor but several identical ones.

La Guardia spent a considerable amount of his seemingly boundless energy fighting for decent housing. Many New Yorkers were living in cramped, dark rooms in squalid tenements without hot water or even indoor toilets. Illnesses were common and child mortality was high. La Guardia didn't live in a tenement, but he had empathy for those living under these conditions: his own daughter had died before reaching her first birthday, and his young wife died of tuberculosis shortly after.

CROTONA PARK POOL [18]
Herbert Magoon, Aymar Embury II
1700 Fulton Ave, Crotona Park East
1937, the Bronx

PCC STREETCARS IN BROOKLYN. In 1936, one hundred new modern trolleys were introduced. While they proved popular with passengers, Mayor Fiorello La Guardia claimed that "trolleys [were] as dead as sailing ships" and blocked any further purchases. They lasted until 1956. In recent years, there have been proposals for streetcars between Brooklyn and Queens. Perhaps it's an idea that is not dead after all.[12]

YELLOW COACH MODEL 720, DOUBLE DECKER. Double-decker buses were a common sight on Fifth Avenue for almost a half a century. This model was nicknamed the Queen Mary in honor of the new, record-breaking ocean liner that traveled direct from London to New York City.[13]

WILLIAMSBURG HOUSES [19]
(Ten Eyck Houses)
Richmond Shereve, William Lescaze
87 Ten Eyck St, Williamsburg
1938, Brooklyn

He helped to push through new building regulations and, most importantly, a new law that finally allowed the city to build its own housing. This was controversial, as some argued housing was better left to the private sector. (The argument continues to this day.) But the fact was that the market was failing to provide sufficient affordable housing, even during the boom years, and so the New York City Housing Association (NYCHA) was established to build and manage city-owned housing.

Surprisingly, the new housing projects weren't for the poor, but rather for people in the lower-middle classes, who had to show a proper income, good housekeeping, and "respectable" behavior to obtain an apartment. Housing was also segregated. Harlem River Houses was built for Black New Yorkers after the 1935 riots shone a light on their hardships and scared city hall into action. A year later, the **WILLIAMSBURG HOUSES [19]** in Brooklyn opened for white families. It wasn't until the late 1940s that public housing became integrated.

The housing in Williamsburg was a radically new design intended to test new ideas, and its successes and failures were to prove influential for decades to come. The neighborhood had some of the most overcrowded blocks in the city and was an ideal place to test

NYCHA's revolutionary plans. They managed to secure twelve neighboring blocks. For the first time ever, the street grid was broken to accommodate housing, creating the "super-block" by merging three regular blocks together. Furthermore, the classic approach of creating enclosed courtyards was replaced with the modernist fashion of individual buildings in open space—what Le Corbusier called "towers in a park." Swiss architect William Lescaze was brought into the project to help with the exteriors and site plan.

Rather than the usual red brick associated with the city's housing, Lescaze chose unconventional light bricks and left the concrete floors to show on the facades. He added oversize windows and spacious corner windows for bedrooms. He also rotated all the buildings by fifteen degrees from the street grid in a typical modernist fashion. But the amount of money spent per apartment proved too high for some critics. Although it was built by the WPA workforce, the housing was finished to a very high standard, with wooden floors, refrigerators, and central heating. Furthermore, the blocks had only four floors and a lot of open park space in between, so the population density was very low.

The inclusion of commercial space was also controversial, as it proved tricky to rent (it was too expensive) and local property owners complained that it created competition. As a result of these grievances, NYCHA did not include commercial space in most of its subsequent developments, and it built higher and kept the construction costs lower. Much lower.

When not promoting public housing, La Guardia was busy endorsing air travel. He served as a pilot in the First World War and saw huge potential in the fast-developing mode of transport. However, flying was still very expensive except to a lucky few. Most of the money from airplanes was actually made from delivering air mail.

Because New York's Floyd Bennett Field in south Brooklyn was so isolated and far from Manhattan, airlines serving the city decided to use New Jersey's Newark airport instead. That meant a new airport closer to Manhattan had to be built. It was decided the runway for the **LAGUARDIA LAND TERMINAL [20]** (originally New York Municipal Airport) should rise from Flushing Bay in Queens. Using WPA funding and workforce, a huge grid of metal frames was fixed in the bay and filled in with soil from subway excavations and garbage from the nearby Rikers Island, which at the time served as the city dump. The steel frames placed under the asphalt interfere with airplane compasses to this day.

To steal airline traffic from Newark, the mayor slashed the landing fees to below cost. It worked, and the airlines brought the city the desired air-mail contract. To capitalize on the public's fascination with air travel, a paid observation deck was built in the terminal. It is hard to comprehend today, but people would willingly spend their free time at the airport watching other people travel. LaGuardia soon became the world's busiest airport. It's very small in comparison with newer airports, and pilots refer to it as "USS *LaGuardia*" because the water-surrounded runway resembles the deck of an aircraft carrier. After years of languishing into what many New Yorkers had dubbed a "hellhole," LaGuardia has recently been given an $8 million refurbishment that has brought it into the 21st century with style.

Situated near the airport was the Corona Ash Dump, a landscape of smoldering ash hills created at a time when most trash was simply burned in incinerators. The 1939 New York World's Fair literally rose from the ashes on the site. Paid for by the big American corporations, the fair—whose theme was "Building the World of Tomorrow"—sought to restore trust in big business and capitalism in general after the excesses of the 1920s resulted in the economic suffering of the Great Depression.

LAGUARDIA LAND TERMINAL [20]
(New York Municipal Airport)
WPA Architects
East Elmhurst
1939-1960s, Queens

NEW YORK MUNICIPAL AIRPORT

WORLD'S FAIR GM FUTURAMA [22]
Norman Bel Geddes
Flushing Meadows Park
1939-1940, Queens

This two-year-long exhibition, with dozens of corporate and national pavilions, was opened by the unlikely trio of President Roosevelt, Mayor La Guardia, and Albert Einstein. The president's speech was broadcast to the grand total of two hundred television sets in the New York area. Food industry exhibitors dispensed tons of free candy to delighted children, whose parents could have rarely afforded such luxury during the Depression.

The fairground's focal point was the **TRYLON & PERISPHERE [21]** designed by Wallace Harrison of Rockefeller Center fame and J. Andre Fouilhoux, a Paris-born engineer and partner of the late Raymond Hood. Inside the Perisphere stood Democracity, a giant model of an ideal metropolis in 2039. Visitors would orbit around it, admiring tiny suburbs cast within a net of wide highways. The city of the future looked an awful lot like Los Angeles.

No building showcased the fair's theme better than the **GM FUTURAMA [22]** pavilion. This stunning streamlined structure was designed by theatrical and industrial designer Norman Bel Geddes. This pavilion also contained a model city of the future, which promised a car-reliant future of superhighways cutting through city centers. It seemed like there was no escape. All the major car manufacturers at the fair and their awesome-looking showrooms overshadowed the more grounded national pavilions.

Sixty foreign governments were represented in structures around the grand concourse, optimistically named Court of Peace, a vain attempt to ignore the fact that the world was on a fast collision course to another war. That autumn, Poland's beautiful pavilion was draped in black cloth after Hitler and Stalin invaded the country.

By the second season of the fair, ten nations didn't reopen their pavilions, mostly because those countries had either been pulled into the war or were under Nazi occupation. By the time the festival gates closed in October 1940, some forty-four million people had visited (somewhat short of the projected one hundred million), but the fair ended in debt (as most fairs do). The futuristic pavilions, so full of promise and optimism, were demolished and their scrap metal used to build weapons for the new war. What remained were happy memories, which many visitors cherished for the rest of their lives.

WORLD'S FAIR TRYLON & PERISPHERE [21]
Wallace Harrison, J. Andre Fouilhoux
Flushing Meadows Park
1939-1940, Queens

BROOKLYN PUBLIC LIBRARY

LIC LIBRARY
OF MUNICIPAL
ITY OFFERS TO ALL
EE ACCESS TO THE
T OF ALL THE AGES

HERE ARE ENSHINED
THE LONGING OF GREAT HEARTS
AND NOBLE THINGS THAT TOWER ABOVE THE TIDE
THE MAGIC WORD THAT WINGED WONDER STARTS
THE GARNERED WISDOM THAT HAS NEVER DIED

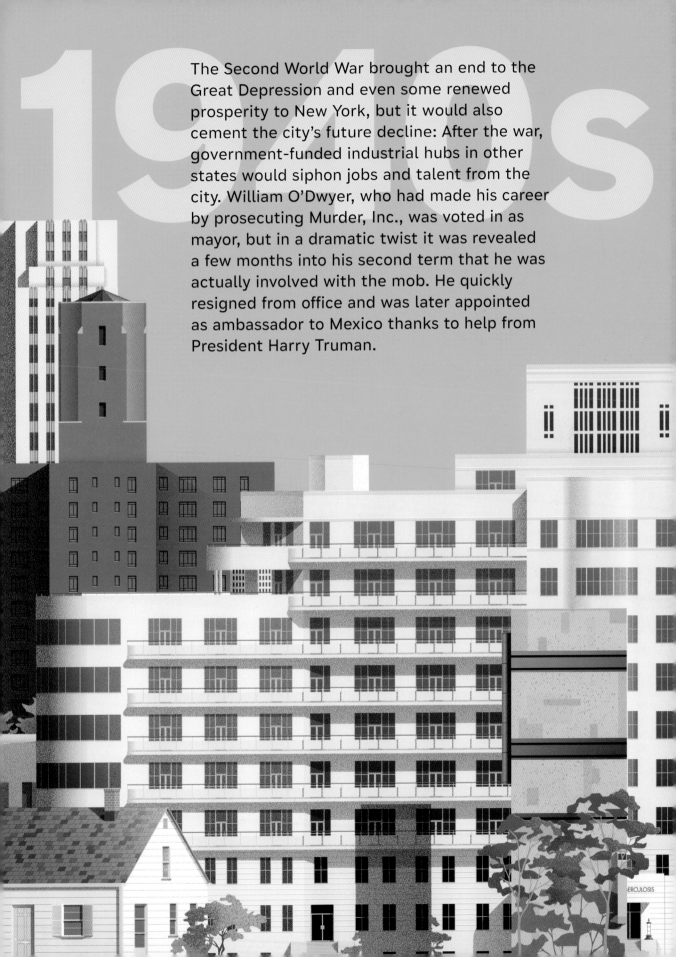

1940s

The Second World War brought an end to the Great Depression and even some renewed prosperity to New York, but it would also cement the city's future decline: After the war, government-funded industrial hubs in other states would siphon jobs and talent from the city. William O'Dwyer, who had made his career by prosecuting Murder, Inc., was voted in as mayor, but in a dramatic twist it was revealed a few months into his second term that he was actually involved with the mob. He quickly resigned from office and was later appointed as ambassador to Mexico thanks to help from President Harry Truman.

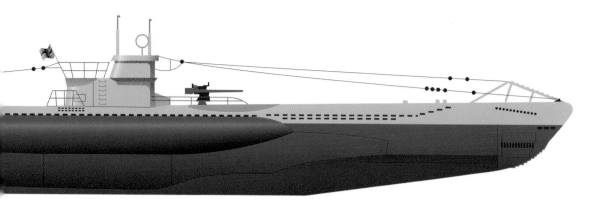

U-202 GERMAN SUBMARINE. One foggy night in 1942, a German U-boat dropped off four secret agents on Amagansett, Long Island. They took an LIRR train into the city, where they seemed to forget about their sabotage mission and instead went drinking. One of them later called the FBI to hand himself over, but they didn't believe him. He had to take a train to FBI headquarters in Washington, DC, where he managed to convince them of his guilt. He was the only one of the four agents to survive the war.

With the end of the 1930s, Americans, including New Yorkers, were nervous. Europe was becoming engulfed in war as the Axis powers crushed nations in their path. By 1940, Great Britain stood alone against the force of Hitler's relentless military machine. Most Americans were opposed to getting involved in what they considered a European war, and many New Yorkers were recent immigrants who traced their ancestors to Ireland, Germany, and Italy, possibly feeling their loyalties being divided.

Scores of Europeans tried to escape to the United States, but the strict immigration quotas meant most were refused entry. People who did manage to flee, mostly the well-connected and wealthy, often decided to remain in New York and join the café society there. One journalist who specialized in writing about high living complained about "rich French refugees with manners which would have outraged a Colorado mining camp."[14]

But when Japan attacked Pearl Harbor on December 7, 1941, sentiments changed. When the shocking news arrived at Rockefeller Center's Time & Life Building, startled journalists scribbled "we are in war with Japan" on paper planes and sent them into the crowds gathered below.[15]

Immediately, the United States was officially at war not only with Japan but also with Germany and Italy. Recruitment offices were swarmed by crowds of young men willing to join the fight. Conversely, as many as seven thousand people—mostly of German, Italian, and Japanese descent or nationality—were sent to Ellis Island for suspected disloyalty to the United States. Yasuo Matsui, architect of 40 Wall Street, was arrested on the night of the attack on Pearl Harbor and then spent the rest of the war on parole.[16]

There was widespread fear that the city would become a target for enemy bombers like in London, the smoking ruins of which were shown in cinema newsreels on repeat. There were thousands of volunteer airplane spotters who watched the skies twenty-four hours a day for enemy planes. Anti-aircraft guns were stationed in the parks around the city. Fortunately, they didn't need to worry as neither German nor Japanese planes had enough range as yet to reach the city.

It was a different story on the high seas, however. New York was the most important port for shipment of men and supplies to Europe, and German submarines sank many ships off the coast. They usually hunted at night, and the light from the shining city made it easy to spot ships on the horizons. To remedy this, residents were ordered to cover windows with a heavy curtain at night, and streetlights and neon signs were dimmed everywhere from Times Square to Coney Island. It was a brownout rather than blackout.

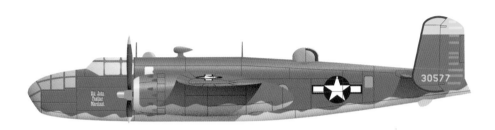

EMPIRE STATE BUILDING, AIR CRASH.
On July 28, 1945, a pilot flying from Bedford, Massachusetts, to Newark, New Jersey, got lost in a thick fog. Confused, he descended way too low and by the time the Empire State Building appeared from the mist it was too late. One of the engines flew into an elevator shaft, cutting the cables and putting the car in freefall. The operator miraculously survived, but three passengers in the B-25 and eleven occupants of the building weren't so lucky.[17]

40 WALL STREET, AIR CRASH. Less than a year after the Empire State Building crash, another air accident happened. A C-45 flying from Louisiana to Newark got lost in fog and hit 40 Wall Street. Five people on the plane perished, but luckily nobody in the building was injured. This was the last such accident until 2006.

MANHATTAN CRIMINAL COURT [23]
(New York County Criminal Court)
Harvey Wiley Corbett, Charles B. Meyers
100 Centre St, Civic Center
1941, Manhattan

The first half of the 1940s was a slow period in terms of new construction, as arming of the country became a priority and building works were stopped. But before that happened, some significant landmarks were completed. **MANHATTAN CRIMINAL COURT [23]** (New York County Criminal Court) was one of those few. It was the first modern government building at the Civic Center, where up to this point courthouses were designed to look like Greek temples and prisons to look like fortresses. But good architecture doesn't need to look to the ancient past to be monumental and respectable.

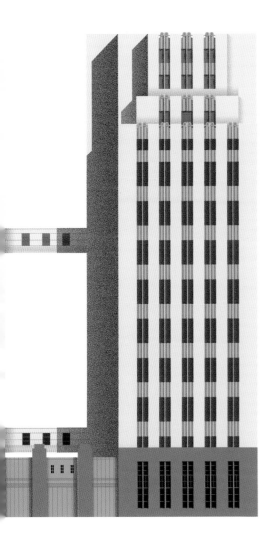

The institution was the oldest criminal court in the country, dating back to the Dutch colony. The new building, sharp and crisp, stood seventeen stories tall and was topped with a ziggurat tower. It was designed by Wiley Corbett (who clearly brought some ideas from his work on Rockefeller Center) and Charles B. Meyers, an expert in municipal buildings. The new structure was split into four connected volumes, one of which—the prison block—stood apart and was connected to the rest only by an overpass called the "Bridge of Sighs."

The opening of the new criminal court coincided with a remarkable drop in serious crime. The number of murders fell to the lowest in the century as military service and plentiful job opportunities steered people away from trouble. The only increased criminal activity was juvenile delinquency, which possibly started when families saw fathers leaving for service and mothers joining the workforce or working for the war cause.

At the time, a married woman was expected to work only in the home, and many single working women were excluded from certain occupations. But mass shortages of workers in every sector caused a sudden shift: Women became cabbies and truck drivers, joined ambulance crews, and later worked in factories and operated heavy machinery. "It's not any harder than housework," one woman noted.[18] Rosie the Riveter became an icon and, eventually, women made up almost a third of the workforce in New York war plants.

Hunter College was one of the biggest women's institutions of higher education at the time. One of its buildings, located on Park Avenue and designed in Gothic fashion, was destroyed by fire in 1936. The college, which was scattered all around Manhattan, used that as an opportunity to centralize into a single building. The charred remains were replaced by a gleaming nineteen-story box. Unusually, the building was stepped back ten feet from the Park Avenue building line, one of the first such gestures seen in New York, but the additional width of the pavement provided little beyond a space for a cigarette break.

The **HUNTER COLLEGE NORTH BUILDING [24]**, designed by the same architects as the Empire State Building, didn't prove particularly popular with the public, who compared it to a warehouse. And they were right: it was a warehouse. But this warehouse was for 5,600 students in 112 classrooms and contained four gyms, an auditorium, and a swimming pool. It was designed as an efficient machine for learning, with a facade free of decoration and large windows that provided plenty of natural light. It was a bold departure for a university at a time when most people equated places of higher learning with the neo-Gothic look of an Ivy League school.

THE RUNAWAY BUS, GM TDH4507. William Cimillo was a Bronx bus driver with sixteen years of experience. One day in 1947, tired of the everyday monotony, Cimillo snapped and just kept driving beyond his normal route. His Bronx local became an express to Florida, some 1,300 miles away. Cimillo was brought back in handcuffs two weeks later but received a hero's welcome from fellow bus drivers, who hosted a dance to raise money for his legal fees. Charges were eventually dropped, and the company even gave him his job back![20]

The US declaration of war brought unprecedented orders of equipment and supplies from the government, divided among the largest American corporations. The torrent of federal cash left the Big Apple dry. The city might have been the country's largest manufacturing center, but its factories were scattered in 27,000 businesses with an average of fifteen employees. Detroit, with its huge automobile plants, received six times more per capita volume of contracts than New York City; San Francisco, Cleveland, and Los Angeles received four times as much.

An incensed Mayor La Guardia went to Washington, DC, and fought for New York City businesses to receive a piece of the action. Gradually, orders arrived: Manhattan's garment industry made uniforms; Bethlehem Steel's shipyard on Staten Island churned out boats; the Queens Steinway Piano Company manufactured Waco gliders; and a former Paramount lot in Astoria was taken over by the Army to shoot instruction movies.

HUNTER COLLEGE NORTH BUILDING [24]
Shreve, Lamb and Harmon
695 Park Ave, Upper East Side
1940, Manhattan

HUNTER COLLEGE

WE ARE OF DIFFERENT OPINIONS
AT DIFFERENT HOURS BUT WE
ALWAYS MAY BE SAID TO BE AT
BOTTOM ON THE...

TRIBORO HOSPITAL FOR
TUBERCULOSIS [25] *(T Building)*
John Russell Pope, Eggers & Higgins
82-41 Parsons Blvd, Jamaica
1941, Queens

In Jamaica, Queens, a new **TRIBORO HOSPITAL FOR TUBERCULOSIS [25]** had just opened. An underground tunnel connected the building with the now-demolished Queens General Hospital. Tuberculosis was once one of the major killers of New Yorkers, and it was thanks to Mayor La Guardia's relentless campaigning that the hospital was built, with almost half of the budget coming from the Public Works Administration (PWA) grants.

Before the age of antibiotics, doctors believed that the sun was the best cure for tuberculosis, and so the new hospital was designed to get as much natural light as possible. The nine-story block was oriented toward the south, and solariums with large glazing were supplemented by lines of balconies and roof terraces where patients could soak up the sun.

If one forgot the reason for the building, it almost seemed like a beach resort. As the method of treating tuberculosis became more sophisticated, the building was converted to a general hospital and later to an administrative building, known as T Building. After sitting empty for years, it has been converted into apartments.

In the early 1940s, everything seemed to be part of the war effort. For example, New Yorkers collected things like silk stockings, which were used for manufacturing parachutes. They started to grow vegetables in parks, on rooftops, and even on fire escapes in tin cans. Abandoned lots were turned into Victory Gardens for extra food. All these activities were promoted by the government to make people more self-sufficient.

People without green fingers could sign up for the gardening course at Brooklyn Botanic Garden. A short walk away stood the brand-new **BROOKLYN CENTRAL LIBRARY [26]**. The borough's library system had stayed independent of the New York Public Library and planning had been in the works for a grand building on par with the Forty-Second Street library ever since 1905. But the usual combination of political intrigue and insufficient funds meant that a quarter of a century later, only one wing of the building had been completed and the design had become notably dated.

Starting anew seemed like a good idea, so the original blueprints were shelved and fresh architects brought in. The classical decoration on the completed wing was chiseled away, and the remaining structure became part of the new building. The unadorned new library would look almost forbidding if it weren't for the gloriously detailed entrance. Two huge pylons frame a forty-foot door decorated with fifteen famous characters from American literature, including Tom Sawyer and Moby Dick. These days the Brooklyn Public Library has some one million users.

BROOKLYN PUBLIC LIBRARY

THE BROOKLYN PUBLIC LIBRARY
THROUGH THE JOINING OF MUNICIPAL
ENTERPRISE AND PRIVATE GENEROSITY OFFERS TO ALL
THE PEOPLE PERPETUAL AND FREE ACCESS TO THE
KNOWLEDGE AND THE THOUGHT OF ALL THE AGES

HERE ARE E
THE LONGING OF G
AND NOBLE THINGS THAT TO
THE MAGIC WORD THAT WIT
THE GARNERED WISDOM IN

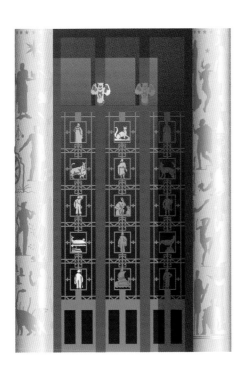

BROOKLYN CENTRAL LIBRARY [26]
Raymond F. Almirall, Francis Keally
10 Grand Army Plaza, Prospect Heights
1941, Brooklyn

Meanwhile, precautions to protect the city from the invasion or attack continued. A giant net was spread between Coney Island and Staten Island's South Beach. The net would be closed every night to block enemy submarines sneaking into the harbor under cover of darkness. Not far from South Beach stands **MILLER FIELD FIRE CONTROL TOWER [27]**, one of the city's few remnants of war infrastructure.

This crude concrete box was once a part of coastal defense protecting the city from seaborne invasion. Its occupants would look through the slits to find targets and radio them to the guns on both sides of the Narrows. Luckily, it was never needed. Miller Army Air Field continued to serve the military until 1969 and in 1972 it became part of Gateway National Recreation Area.

MILLER FIELD FIRE CONTROL TOWER [27]
Army Corps of Engineers
Miller Field, New Dorp
1943, Staten Island

Camp Shanks in Orangetown was the Army's largest embarkation camp, the last stop before ships took the troops to Europe or Africa. Some 1.3 million men went through there, and they usually got a twenty-four-hour pass to enjoy their last bit of freedom. Most headed to Times Square, where theaters and nightclubs were permanently crowded. The Stage Door Canteen, where everything was free of charge for uniformed servicemen and servicewomen, was an alternative to dive bars, serving only nonalcoholic drinks and sandwiches. As an added attraction, the canteen was staffed by stars from theater, radio, and film, all of whom volunteered their time.

And it was in Times Square that people celebrated the end of the war in 1945. After four years, people were determined to move on. As one wartime advertisement promised, "After Total War Total Living." But this wasn't the case for everyone, of course. To provide jobs for returning GIs, businesses started to cut staff: women and Black workers were first to go. Providing returnees with housing, however, would prove an even greater challenge.

At that time, the Metropolitan Life Insurance Company, the largest private corporation in America, insured a third of all city-dwelling Americans.[21] Replacing slums with new housing was a sensible investment: Improved living conditions decreased claims on life insurance, and the company could then reap profits from the real estate. So, MetLife built Riverton Houses in Harlem with 1,232 units. And in 1942 they completed the more than 12,000-unit Parkchester in the Bronx, the largest housing project in the country. Because there was a long-term shortage of housing in New York, city hall went out of its way to support such ventures with economic incentives like tax exemptions.

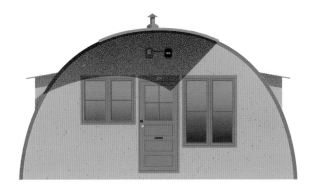

QUONSET HUTS. A colony of temporary housing for 2,000 families of war veterans was built in Canarsie, Brooklyn, along the Belt Parkway, using surplus Army Quonset huts. Made of corrugated metal sheets, the huts leaked and were hard to keep warm in winter. In the mid-1950s, most of them were cleared away; some were sold for use as garages or storage units; some survive to this day scattered around the borough.[22]

The new **STUYVESANT TOWN [28]** (now known as Stuyvesant Town-Peter Cooper Village) was built with war veterans and their new families in mind. Only white, married couples could get on the waiting lists. Soon, thousands of babies were born and the development became known as "Rabbit Town." From the outside, the austere thirteen-story blocks looked similar to low-income housing, but the apartments were much bigger and had high-quality finishes. The blocks themselves form a wall around the boundary of the site and then circle around a central oval. Bleak at first, the area became beautiful once the trees matured.

Stuy Town construction provided an early preview of issues linked with so-called slum clearance. Some 11,000 people were living in the Gas House District when the city declared it as blighted and razed it to make way for the new development. Of the dislocated families, barely 3 percent could afford the rent in the new buildings, while only 22 percent were eligible for public housing. The majority were from the lower-middle class with income too high for public assistance and too low for new private housing in the area.

STUYVESANT TOWN [28] *(Stuy Town)*
Gilmore Clark, Irwin Clavan,
H. F. Richardson, George Gore,
Andrew Eken
252 1st Ave, Stuyvesant Town
1949, Manhattan

Some families moved out of the city altogether and out to the suburbs, taking advantage of cheap, government-subsidized mortgages being offered. The most significant of the new suburbs was **LEVITTOWN [29]** on Long Island. It was built by William Levitt & Sons, who applied the skills gained in building temporary housing for the US Navy. The company separated the whole process of house construction into twenty-seven steps, with each step to be completed by different subcontractors. Levitt & Sons bought whole forests and a lumber mill, made their own nails, and dealt directly with manufacturers of home appliances to avoid markup.

The pace of construction was dizzying, and Levitt & Sons sometimes built as many as thirty-six two-bedroom houses per day. By 1951, more than 17,000 Levitt houses had sprouted on what had been Long Island's onion and potato fields. Where some saw tidiness and neatness, others saw oppressive uniformity as thousands of nearly identical houses with neatly trimmed lawns stretched for miles. (If you left your grass too long, the company gardener would mow it and leave a bill in the mailbox.)

The model proved so successful that the company replicated Levittown in New Jersey, Pennsylvania, and Puerto Rico. It inspired countless similar suburbs that surround every US city today.

LEVITT CAPE COD [29]
William Levitt & Sons
Levittown, Hempstead
1947, Long Island

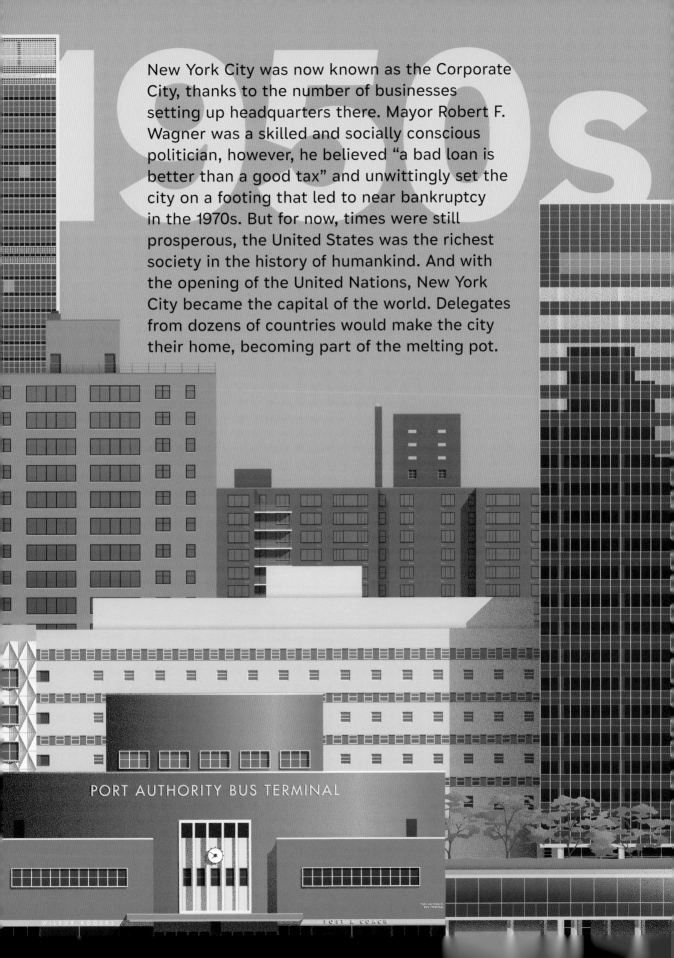

New York City was now known as the Corporate City, thanks to the number of businesses setting up headquarters there. Mayor Robert F. Wagner was a skilled and socially conscious politician, however, he believed "a bad loan is better than a good tax" and unwittingly set the city on a footing that led to near bankruptcy in the 1970s. But for now, times were still prosperous, the United States was the richest society in the history of humankind. And with the opening of the United Nations, New York City became the capital of the world. Delegates from dozens of countries would make the city their home, becoming part of the melting pot.

PORT AUTHORITY BUS TERMINAL

New York's garment industry was the biggest in the country but, in terms of fashion, it largely depended on styles coming out of Paris. It was only during the Second World War, when France was under occupation, that American designers were given a chance to shine and innovate. The Fashion Institute of Technology (FIT) was founded to be "the MIT for fashion" and to bring fresh blood to an industry that had struggled to attract young, ambitious people.

In 1959, FIT moved to their first true home in the heart of Chelsea's garment district. The building now known as the **FASHION INSTITUTE OF TECHNOLOGY FELDMAN CENTER [30]** was designed by De Young, Moscowitz & Rosenberg. The architects clad the building in fancy origami-like aluminum panels.

They weren't afraid to use color, and so the panels were in a shade of bronze and the windows in complementary gold frames. The building was originally designed for 1,200 students but was soon bursting at the seams: Four years later, there were already three times as many students.

By 1979, when New York's fashion status rose to be comparable to Paris or Milan, the FIT campus had six more buildings and encompassed the whole block. Each building was built in the up-to-the-minute style and, as a result, aged unusually fast. Architecture critics drew the obvious parallel between the worlds of fashion and architecture. The campus today feels like an architectural walking tour of styles from midcentury modern to brutalism.

FASHION INSTITUTE OF TECHNOLOGY FELDMAN CENTER [30]
(Marvin Feldman Center and the Business and Liberal Arts Center)
De Young, Moscowitz & Rosenberg
227 W 27th St, Midtown
1959, Manhattan

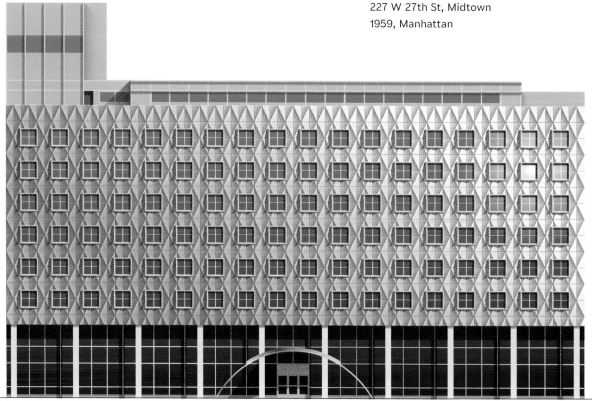

**THE NEW YORK PORT
AUTHORITY BUS TERMINAL**
[31] *(Authority Bus Terminal)*
Port Authority Architects
625 8th Ave, Midtown
1950, Manhattan

Since the opening of the Lincoln Tunnel, which connected New Jersey with Manhattan, in 1937, West Midtown had been where a number of terminals for interstate buses became located. Everyday thousands of buses, mainly carrying commuters from across the Hudson, created traffic chaos in the streets. Plans for a single, all-encompassing terminal had been floated for years, but were stalled because of the Second World War and Robert Moses's disdain of mass transit.

But finally, construction began after a rooftop parking lot for five hundred cars was added to the original terminal design. **THE NEW YORK PORT AUTHORITY BUS TERMINAL [31]**, architecturally bland but technically impressive, opened in 1950. A series of ramps connected it straight to the Lincoln Tunnel entrance, keeping buses off the surrounding streets completely. The ramps, steep and curvy, were heated in the winter to melt snow and ice.

It was considered the most efficient bus terminal in the world, and you could buy a ticket there to any place in the country.

Over the years the terminal was upgraded, but mostly in terms of capacity, rather than the comfort of the travelers. In 1963, three new decks of parking lots were built on the roof, and in 1979 a new wing opened, doubling the size of the whole building. The original terminal was united with the new addition by a menacingly dark facade made of X-shaped steel trusses.

In the 1970s, the proximity to the then-seedy Times Square, disregard for maintenance, and lack of law enforcement gradually turned the terminal into a dangerous cesspit to be avoided. The late 1990s brought some improvements, but the terminal remains a black hole where time and space deform. "If hell had hell, that would be it," commented one Hoboken commuter.

But in 1951 the horrific scenes weren't just on the traffic-clogged streets—an exhibition by the Civil Defense Commission at the terminal featured a large mural of Manhattan after an atomic bomb had been dropped on it. (Not the most uplifting thing to see while commuting.) The Cold War was beginning to heat up and the mural was just one of many informational campaigns that sought to educate (and scare) citizens about the prospect of a nuclear attack.

Another war seemed inevitable, and the Big Apple was seen as a juicy target. Civil defense drills were held and fallout shelters built. City schoolchildren were even issued dog tags so their bodies could be identified in the case of an attack. Children were also shown an animated film featuring Bert the Turtle, who taught them to "duck and cover" in case of a nuclear explosion.

But after the ravages of the Second World War, fifty-one Member States had come together to form an organization designed to prevent any future wars: The United Nations (UN). The UN was founded in San Francisco in 1945 with a vision of global peacekeeping but finding the right location for the **UNITED NATIONS HEADQUARTERS [32]** proved to be the first hurdle. New York City was eventually settled on. The UN was given temporary headquarters in Flushing Meadows, Queens, in a building left over from the World's Fair.

The Manhattan site for the UN was gifted by the Rockefeller family, who had bought the property from William Zeckendorf, a major developer whose plan for the site had potential to become a competition to Rockefeller Center. The six city blocks in Turtle Bay (no relation to Bert the Turtle) were occupied chiefly by slaughterhouses and tenements and were separated from the East River by the busy FDR Drive. A deck was constructed to hide the roadway and enlarge the site.

UNITED NATIONS HEADQUATRES [32]
Le Corbusier and others
405 E 42nd St, Turtle Bay
1952, Manhattan

An international team of architects—from Australia, Belgium, Brazil, Canada, China, France, the Soviet Union, Sweden, the United Kingdom, and Uruguay—was headed by Wallace K. Harrison, the Rockefeller family's personal architect. Harrison also had a personal connection to Robert Moses, whose help would be essential. But the heavy-hitter of the team was undoubtedly Charles-Édouard Jeanneret, known as Le Corbusier. Representing Brazil, Oscar Niemeyer also made a significant contribution to the design and aesthetics.

The complex design needed to feel as if it belonged to all nations, and so had to avoid aesthetics linked to any one culture. With its sleek lines and practical application of modern materials, International Style was agreed on. Le Corbusier, whose work helped to define the whole modernist movement, influenced the final design the most. But his considerable ego didn't allow him to be part of the team, and Harrison struggled to keep Le Corbusier from destroying the idea of international teamwork.

The headquarters had three main elements, the most notable was the thirty-nine-story Secretariat Building. Its facades were completely clad in blue-green glass. This glazing was somewhat heat-absorbing (not by today's standards), but so much air-conditioning machinery was necessary that whole floors were taken over by it. Interestingly, these floors weren't hidden in the design, but just the opposite—the gridded intakes on these floors helped break up the glass cladding and functioned as kind of mechanical decoration.

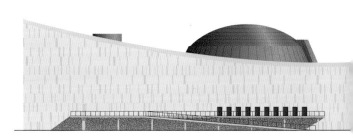

In contrast to the lightness of the glass curtain wall were the north/south elevations. Nothing, not a single window or seatback, broke the solid mass of marble. From certain angles, the building looked like a giant ancient monolith.

The least visible of the three main elements was the Conference Building, which was mostly hidden from First Avenue behind the Secretariat. As the name suggests, the building contained three large conference rooms, each designed by architects from Denmark, Norway, and Sweden. The last, and most playful of the buildings, was the General Assembly, where the main proceedings would happen. The dramatically shaped structure brought dynamism to the site. It was originally set to be clad in marble, but a less expensive alternative—Portland stone from England—was found.

Traffic problems began to grow as an increased number of suburban commuters—encouraged by newer, ever-widening roads—drove their cars to Manhattan. There was simply not enough space to park them; double- and triple-parked cars created gridlocks all over Manhattan. In 1951, the City Planning Commission began recommending that new developments include off-street parking. In residential construction, that didn't usually lead to garage building but rather to "towers-in-the-carpark." Surface parking replaced green space in the ultimate deformation of Le Corbusier's dream of high-rises in lush landscape.

Such was the case with **PARK WEST VILLAGE [33]**, a set of slab buildings surrounding a large parking lot. But the development has a darker history than just bad use of space. It started life as Manhattantown in 1952, when Moses handed over the six crowded blocks to developers. It was a Title I project, an attempt to motivate private investors to construct more affordable housing. The usual process was that the city would condemn a number of run-down blocks in otherwise desirable neighborhoods and give them to a developer. The developer would in turn receive a federally backed loan to tear the buildings down and replace them with housing for the middle class.

CROSS BRONX PARKWAY. This seven-mile roadway wasn't built along an established route or shoreline but cut directly through established neighborhoods, which destroyed communities and displaced sixty thousand people, mostly lower- and middle-class Jews, Germans, and Irish. The parkway is considered as one of the major causes for the decline of the Bronx. Autocratic Robert Moses refused to consider an alternative route a few blocks away that would cause a fraction of the damage. It is all documented in Robert Caro's 1974 biography of Moses, The Power Broker.

PARK WEST VILLAGE [33]
(Manhattantown)
Melvin Kessler, Skidmore Owings & Merrill
788 Columbus Ave, Upper West Side
1957, Manhattan

Theoretically, limits on maximum profits were set, but there were many ways to milk the system, like overstating the money needed for construction and pocketing the difference. But in the case of Manhattantown things were even worse: The investors never even began the redevelopment and just collected the rents without spending a dime on maintenance. And, in addition, they siphoned off federal money through multiple schemes. This went on for five years.

Moses had relied on the support of wealthy background players who called the shots down at city hall. To please them, he would give them sweet deals that brought considerable profits—usually at taxpayer expense.

When a Senate banking commission began investigating Manhattantown, things finally got moving. The shady investors were let off the hook without any punishment, but they and others involved (including the architect) were banned from participating in future Title I projects. The site was then handed over to a new developer, Zeckendorf, who didn't waste any time: He paid the back taxes owed by the previous developers, renamed the project (which had become infamous by that point), and brought in Skidmore Owings & Merrill (SOM) to polish the design. By 1959, the first three buildings were built, with another four to come.

As the Cold War continued into the late 1950s, the government propaganda machine promoting the virtues of US capitalism and democracy and highlighting the corruption of the Soviet system was in full gear. However, the Soviets were well within their rights to criticize the so-called Land of the Free when racial minorities in the United States were segregated and treated like second-class citizens. When the successful, integrated **NORTH QUEENSVIEW HOMES [34]** opened in Queens, the development was proudly shown to a Soviet housing delegation touring the city.

But it was the residents, rather than the government, that turned Queensview into a true achievement. The fact that the homes were racially integrated from the start brought many progressive families, mainly Jewish but also some Italian and Greek, from places like Greenwich Village or the West Bronx. The families went on to organize a nursery school, a variety of clubs, and many communal activities that would continue for decades to come.

The project was initially intended for the "forgotten" families, those whose income was too high to be eligible for NYCHA apartments but not high enough to afford new market-rate housing. The housing was arranged as a limited equity cooperative for those in the lower-middle income bracket. Residents purchased shares in the development—rather than individual units—and agreed to sell only at a price determined by a formula to maintain affordability over the long term.

From a distance, Queensview looked just like another of dozens of low-income housing projects rising around town. The main difference was inside: there were only four apartments per floor, each with windows facing two directions that guaranteed plenty of light and fresh air. Baseboard heating allowed for oversize windows that started lower to the floor than usual.

To allow for such luxuries, the architects eliminated basements and moved storage and offices to the ground floor. Laundry and outdoor play space were on the roof. If the Soviets were impressed by Queensview, they didn't show it. "There's too many individual TV aerials, you should have a big communal antenna like in Moscow," was one comment according to the *New York Times*.

But while only a handful of Muscovites actually owned a television set (there was only one channel anyway), Americans embraced TV as a part of daily life. People grew more isolated in the suburbs and television became a part of the family. Visits to cinemas and libraries declined, and restaurants suffered as TV dinners became popular. Products promoted on television saw a huge rise in sales, leading to a revolution in advertising. The Madison Avenue "Mad Men" led the charge.

TAXI, FORD CUSTOM 300. In the 1950s, while industrial unions around the city organized workers into factions with economic and political power, taxi drivers (or hacks, as they called themselves) were left behind. Their union was run by mobsters, and there were divisions between the independent, car-owning drivers and the ones driving for cab companies. Some of these fleets had vivid color schemes in an effort to stand out among the sea of yellow vehicles.

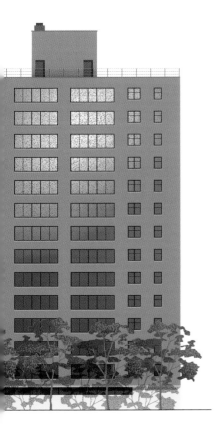

**NORTH QUEENSVIEW
HOMES [34]**
Brown & Guenther
33-60 21st St, Astoria
1950, Queens

Proximity to the big advertising agencies became one of the main reasons that the nation's corporations began their move to New York City. For example, the reason that the soap-producing Lever Brothers settled on Park Avenue rather than elsewhere was because, as a company representative once said, "The price one pays for soap is 89 percent advertisement [...] and the advertising agencies of America were there."

LEVER HOUSE [35], their new building, redefined office architecture. It was designed by Gordon Bunshaft and Natalie de Blois of SOM. Given the cost of Manhattan land, corporations usually built their headquarters as big as planning would allow, renting any excess space to other companies. But Lever Brothers was different. They wanted the headquarters all to themselves. Charles Luckman, president of the corporation, had been an architect and promoted the new building as a chance to heighten the status of the company.

The building was unique in many ways. Its footprint consisted of only a glass reception area and a series of columns—the rest was open space. Above this hovered a single-story box structure that contained mailrooms and stock rooms and had a garden on its roof. A vertical slab on its northern edge contained the actual offices.

Taking part in the building process rekindled Luckman's love of architecture, and he quit as Lever Brothers president even before the building was completed. He dusted off his drawing tools and restarted his career in architecture. He teamed up with his old friend, William Pereira, and moved to Los Angeles.

VERTOL 44B. America's first helicopter airline, New York Airways, began operating flights at 90-minute intervals between LaGuardia, Idlewild Airport (now JFK), and Newark airports in 1953. In 1958 it began using the Vertol-44, called the "flying banana," whose interior more resembled that of an airplane and could accommodate fifteen passengers. They were fitted with inflatable floats in case of an emergency landing in the East or Hudson Rivers. Other stops included helipads on West Thirtieth Street in Manhattan, Bridgeport, Connecticut, and Teterboro, New Jersey. New York Airways operated its last flight in 1979.

LEVER HOUSE [35]
Gordon Bunshaft and
Natalie de Blois of SOM
390 Park Ave, Midtown
1952, Manhattan

New York became known as the company headquarters town of the United States and big business came in droves. Even Seagram, Canada's biggest whisky distillery, decided to take up residence in the city. Keen to follow the triumph of the Lever House, Seagram picked a site literally across the street and, just to be sure, asked Luckman to be their architect. Success seemed guaranteed.

In 1954, Phyllis Lambert, the recently divorced daughter of Seagram's CEO, was living in Paris and received a letter from her father with a sketch of the proposed building headquarters. Horrified, she immediately penned him an eight-page, single-spaced letter with the words "NO NO NO NO NO" in block letters at the top. Seagram got the hint and took his daughter's advice, delegating her to find a replacement architect.[23]

Enter Mies van der Rohe, a German emigre of already legendary status known for his clear, minimalistic designs and now-iconic sayings "Less is more" and "God is in the details." For the Seagram Building he designed a simple, dark, unadorned tower with a perfectly proportioned grid of bronze mullions and bronze-tinted windows, all joined by refined technical details.

DON'T WALK SIGN. New signs were installed at Times Square in 1952 in an attempt to lower the number of pedestrians mowed down by drivers. The word WALK in green neon was always lit, while the word DONT in red was switched on and off with the traffic cycle. It was confusing, and so a new, more comprehensive model was introduced three years later.[25]

What proved to be revolutionary was the decision to create a plaza in front of the tower, but not a small one like in front of Hunter College or the walk-through space beneath Lever House. This would be a substantial expanse of open, unused space in the heart of the most expensive city in the world. Van der Rohe designed the plaza so that pedestrians on the street could see the building properly, without an unobstructed view.

There were no benches and only two fountains that would always be filled to the brim (per van der Rohe's instructions) so that people couldn't sit on the edge. Beyond that, the whole border of the site was made for sitting and, on sunny days, catching some rays. The **SEAGRAM BUILDING [36]** became an instant classic and was an inspiration for the new 1961 zoning laws, which allowed developers to build taller structures in exchange for creating plaza space in front.[24] However, few other plazas would ever be as successful, and most became empty and windswept eyesores that broke the street line.

SEAGRAM BUILDING [36]
Ludwig Mies van der Rohe, Philip Johnson
375 Park Ave, Midtown
1958, Manhattan

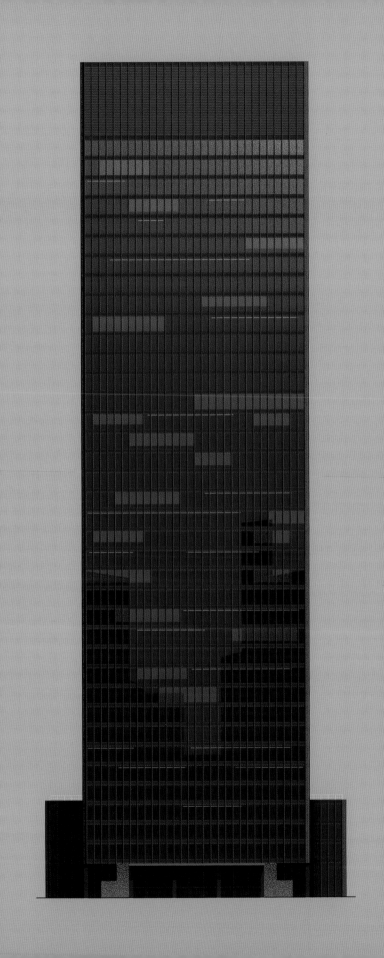

Frank Lloyd Wright, considered the greatest American architect of all time, was notably absent from New York City. He disliked it intensely. Like many other notable architects of the time, he was generally anti-urban and dreamed about creating new cities from scratch. But when a commission for the **SOLOMON R. GUGGENHEIM MUSEUM [37]** came up, he couldn't resist. It took Wright thirteen long years to find the right site and design, going through many phases, including one version with a pink facade.

The building was so unusual that Robert Moses, who was related to Wright by marriage, had to push it through the planning process to get the approval. When planning officers highlighted inadequate fire safety and structural issues, Wright took it personally and attacked them in the press, accusing them of obstructing great art.

A genius with an ego to match, Wright drummed up public support and positioned the museum as a heroic building. Meanwhile local architect Arthur Cort Holden was hired and worked in the background to smooth out any issues.

The museum became a favorite spot for visitors and locals alike. Its distinctive spiral ramp, at three quarters of a mile in length, is an unforgettable experience. When a museum's design is so powerful, it can get in the way of its main function—providing a neutral space to enjoy art without distraction. But the Guggenheim's architecture is so iconic that it nevertheless attracts art lovers in droves.

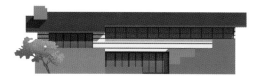

THE CRIMSON BEECH (CASS HOUSE). Built in Staten Island's Lighthouse Hill neighborhood for the Cass family, the prefabricated ranch house is New York City's only residential structure by Frank Lloyd Wright. Wright didn't live to see either Cass House, completed in 1959, or the Guggenheim Museum finished. He died just short, on April 9, 1959, at age 91, following an incredibly rich career of more than seventy years.

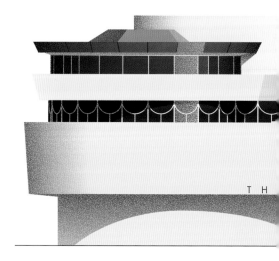

**SOLOMON R. GUGGENHEIM
MUSEUM [37]**
Frank Lloyd Wright
1071 Fifth Ave,
Upper East Side
1959, Manhattan

The Brooklyn-Battery tunnel (recently rechristened the Hugh L. Carey Tunnel after the former governor) finally opened in 1950. With a length of 1.7 miles, it stayed the world's longest for fifty years. There are two ventilation towers in Manhattan, one in Brooklyn, and one on Governors Island to keep fresh air circulating. At the same time, streetcar tracks were removed from the Brooklyn Bridge and the space was given to cars and buses.

With this new connection, Brooklyn's downtown was now in urban renewal's crosshairs. The Civic Center, dating back to the borough's independence, was completely remodeled. The new focal point of the area became Cadman Plaza, a grassy mall that stretched from the Brooklyn Bridge to Borough Hall (which used to serve as Brooklyn's City Hall until consolidation with the city). More than three hundred buildings and thousands of industrial jobs disappeared in the process that brought new civic monuments and middle-class housing.

One of these new buildings was the **NEW YORK STATE SUPREME COURT [38]** (also known as Kings County Supreme Court), which was quickly and harshly dubbed, "the ugliest building in America" by author Leslie Katz, who commented that it "looks curiously incomplete, ribbons of black stone joining the windows, a gigantic flower pot without flowers." Its windows were so unusually small that it seemed to be designed to stop anyone wanting to jump out in desperation.

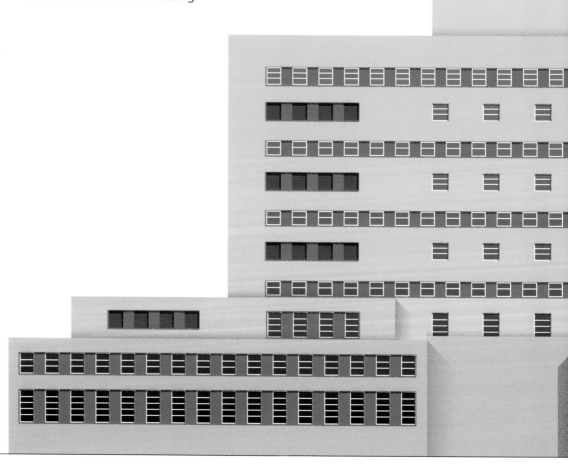

NEW YORK STATE SUPREME COURT
[38] *(Kings County Supreme Court)*
Shreve, Lamb and Harmon
360 Adams Street, Downtown Brooklyn
1957, Brooklyn

TROLLEYBUS. Using overhead wires left over from Brooklyn streetcars, trolleybuses were fast, comfortable, and didn't pollute the air. They served on a handful of lines for three decades. The last trolleybus reached its destination in 1960, just four years after the last streetcar.

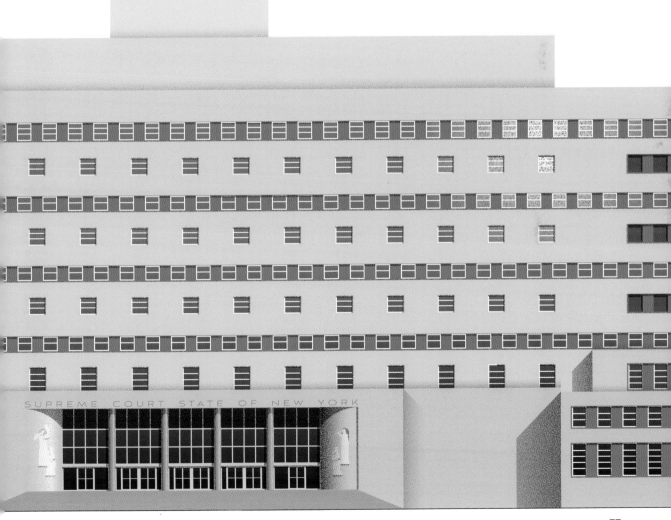

SUPREME COURT STATE OF NEW YORK

The 1960s was a decade of optimism, hope, and violence. New Yorkers were ready for something new and in 1966 voted in John V. Lindsay as mayor. Youthful and with Hollywood looks, Lindsay's campaign slogan was, "He is fresh and everyone else is tired." He brought along many young and idealistic people, many who helped to modernize city hall and improve the plight of minorities. But crime kept rising, cracks in financing appeared, and residents of the outer boroughs felt ignored. Lindsay's remark about New York being "Fun City" was much quoted, although sarcastically.

1960s

Optimism. That's what Cyprus-born Costas Machlouzarides communicated through the colorful facade of **THE GREATER REFUGE TEMPLE [39]** near 125th Street in Harlem. Originally a popular ballroom built in the late 19th century, Harlem Casino was gutted and rebuilt in an audacious way. But not everything old could be overhauled so completely. Railroads, once a cutting-edge business, were facing new circumstances.

The number of train passengers dropped as competition rose. The fast-growing network of highways was built with government money, making car and bus journeys faster and more comfortable. At the same time, air travel boomed and airlines used municipal airports, which paid no tax. In contrast, Pennsylvania Station and Grand Central Terminal cost their operators millions in property taxes and maintenance.

It was a cold business decision to sell Penn Station for redevelopment: The railroad company would keep the underground levels (where most of the operation happened) and get a 25 percent stake in the replacement development. New Yorkers, disturbed by the demolition of several historic buildings during the latest office construction boom, took to the streets. The public protests were joined by celebrities like Norman Mailer, Philip Johnson, and Paul Rudolph, but to no avail.

THE GREATER REFUGE TEMPLE [39]
Costas Machlouzarides
2081 Adam Clayton Powell, Jr. Blvd, Harlem
1966, Manhattan

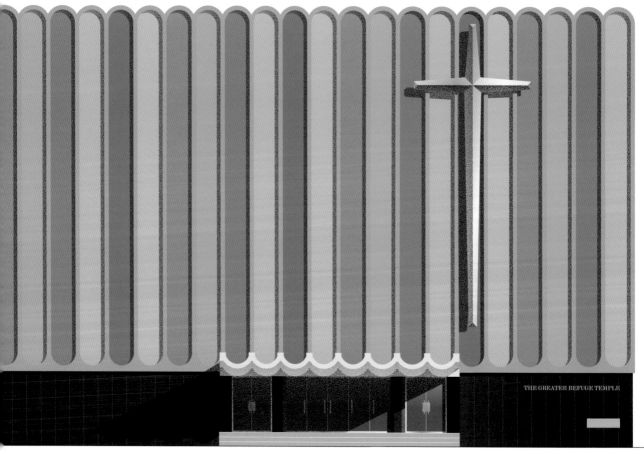

THE GREATER REFUGE TEMPLE

MADISON SQUARE GARDEN [40]

Charles Luckman
4 Pennsylvania Plaza, Midtown
1968, Manhattan

The demolition of this icon shocked the city and became a rallying point for the introduction of the New York City Landmarks Law in 1965, intended to protect such buildings. Most of beautiful Penn Station wound up in a dump at New Jersey's Meadowlands, but fragments survived—twenty-two eagle sculptures from the facade found new nesting sites as far away as Kansas City and Philadelphia. Two others remained outside the subway entrance on Seventh Avenue.

The station's replacement was probably the best example of multilayered building since the Downtown Athletic Club. Above the busiest train station in the country rose **MADISON SQUARE GARDEN [40]**, a giant multipurpose venue with 20,000 seats, a cinema, a forty-eight-lane bowling alley, and a conference hall. While an attractive prospect on paper in cut-away drawings, the reality was less exciting—it was a concrete-clad hatbox sitting next to another similarly graceless slab.

The new train station, tucked away in the lower levels, was claustrophobic and depressing. Yale professor and architecture historian Vincent J. Scully best summarized the change in feeling for the commuter: "One entered the city like a god; one scuttles in now like a rat."

R-32 SUBWAY TRAINS. Built in Philadelphia by the Budd Company, the R-32 subway trains served the city for more than half a century, longer than any other model. They were nicknamed "Brightliners" for their shiny, ribbed stainless steel skin that resembled a washboard. On January 1, 1966, Mayor Lindsay's first day in office, the first city-wide transit strike started. The chaos lasted for twelve days until the mayor capitulated and agreed to the transit union's demands.

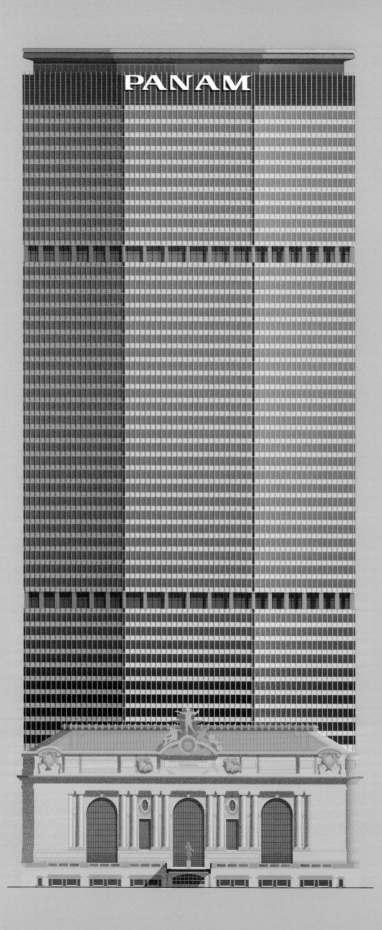

In Midtown, Grand Central was in a similar situation as Penn Station. The railroad company deferred maintenance and stuffed the interior with intrusive advertising but was still losing money. Rising property prices around Park Avenue inevitably led to plans to exploit the air rights above the terminal. Luckily, plans to demolish the station's Grand Concourse were abandoned after a sustained campaign by people like Jackie Kennedy Onassis. What was built instead was the **PANAM BUILDING [41]** (now MetLife Building), which stands between the station and New York Central Building.

Emery Roth & Sons designed an unremarkable humongous slab for the site. The developer, aware of the growing backlash against their so-called Rothscrapers—which the prolific architects produced in the dozens every year—decided to bring in some flashier names to increase the chances of attracting investors. These were the architects/academics German emigre Walter Gropius, chairman of Harvard Architecture Department, and Italian-born Pietro Belluschi, dean at MIT.

The last time academic Gropius, legendary founder of Bauhaus, had designed a tall building was probably in 1922 for the Chicago Tribune Tower competition (which Raymond Hood won). But Gropius jumped at the opportunity and was involved much more than was expected.

He and Belluschi shaved off the sides from Roth's tower plan and made it into an elongated octagon. This reduced the mass by 20 percent and made it appear slightly less bulky, but the effect was lost when Gropius decided to change the orientation of the tower, supposedly for more efficient air conditioning. Originally designed to stand with its narrow side aligned with Park Avenue, the new orientation effectively turned the building into a giant dam that forever blocked off one of the world's most impressive urban views.

PANAM BUILDING [41]
(MetLife Building)
Walter Gropius, Pietro Belluschi,
Emery Roth & Sons
200 Park Ave, Midtown
1963, Manhattan

BOEING-VERTOL V107. The helicopter, a replacement for the "flying bananas," had an extra engine to provide additional safety for flying over the city. The V107 was later developed into the famous Chinook. The whirlybirds connected the helipad at the PanAm Building with every major airport in the area and were operated by New York Airways, although some sported PanAm colors.

The *New York Times* architecture critic Ada Louise Huxtable, who was a pioneer as the first at a US newspaper, described the building charitably as "gigantically second-rate." Gropius, once considered one of the fathers of modernism, was now ironically one of its gravediggers: The building was seen by some as a bitter end of the movement. Decades later when *New York* magazine polled one hundred prominent New Yorkers on which building they would love to see torn down, the MetLife Building won hands-down. (Some probably cheered when the bad-tempered radioactive lizard smashed a hole through it in 1994's *Godzilla*.)

The original tenant, Pan American World Airlines, or PanAm as it was known, was the most powerful American airline for half a century. Fittingly, the company had a helipad installed on the roof—the highest in the world. Well-heeled travelers could check in right in Midtown and enjoy a cocktail before being flown to the airport, where they would be ushered straight to a waiting jet.

The helicopter ride took only seven minutes to John F. Kennedy International Airport (JFK), originally Idlewild and renamed after the president's 1963 assassination, in Queens. JFK was the second municipal airport after LaGuardia, and its construction required immense resources: So much sand was used to reclaim the land from the marshes that it could cover every street in Manhattan eight feet deep. LaGuardia Airport, which operated at full capacity just a year after opening, was now relegated to short-haul flights, while JFK took over longer and international routes.

CHECKER A11/12. *Sturdy and with a lot of room in the back, the design became iconic and remained almost unchanged for the 20 years of production. From 1970 all Gotham's medallion taxis had to be yellow, putting an end to the multicolored liveries many of them used to don. Bulletproof partitions also became mandatory, as robberies and violence claimed cabbies.*[26]

TWA FLIGHT CENTER [42]
(TWA Hotel)
Eero Saarinen
1 Idlewild Drive, JFK
International Airport
1962, Queens

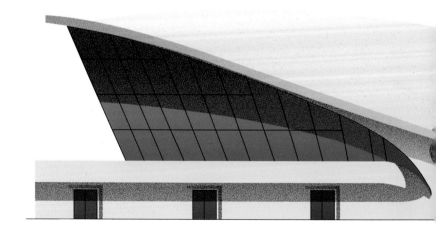

Airlines decided to build their own terminals as a way of increasing their customer appeal; this was one of the few ways to attract customers in times when air travel was heavily standardized (ticket prices were set by the government, etc.). Trans World Airlines, or TWA, was controlled by eccentric millionaire Howard Hughes and was second only to PanAm. (However, it was in a shaky position as it was slow to obtain jet airliners.)

TWA now wanted to fully embrace the jet age and hired Finnish American architect Eero Saarinen, who could do magic with reinforced concrete. Saarinen had also designed the famous Gateway Arch in St. Louis, Missouri. His **TWA FLIGHT CENTER [42]** (now TWA Hotel) was unconventional in every sense of the word. Along with Kevin Roche and engineers Ammann & Whitney, Saarinen worked closely with the builders to make the construction as economical as possible. They came up with a clever way to use straight section boards in the formwork for the poured concrete.

Still, TWA was financially ailing, and cuts had to be made to the design. Regardless, it was a remarkable success when it opened and overshadowed other terminals at JFK. (Although critics pointed out that the terminal didn't really look like a bird in flight as the design was supposed to but rather like a horseshoe crab.) Boarding was done via wings extending from the terminal, a more practical solution than PanAm's circular Worldport, which could not be easily extended.

Both TWA and PanAm eventually landed at bankruptcy courts as the air travel entered a new, less flamboyant era. TWA Terminal was luckily preserved and repurposed as a cool hotel, a fate other transportation buildings didn't have. On the other side of Queens, in Flushing Meadows, the World's Fair came back after twenty-five years. Robert Moses was appointed to lead it as his retirement gift; he was finally being ousted from city government after years of scandals. Now his interest was mainly in transforming Flushing Meadows into a park as his final legacy, and he saw the fair as a way of making the needed cash to pay for it. Everything was focused on the bottom line.

Rents for the exhibitors were hiked up sky-high, and the layout of the old 1939 fair was reused to save on landscaping. But the high-handed Moses was unable to respect the Paris-based World's Fair commission and insulted them in the media. As a result, the commission instructed the member countries to avoid New York. Most cooperated, and so only a handful of national pavilions were built, with the rest coming from corporations. The fair's lofty motto, "Peace through Understanding," sounded hollow, as there were so few nations represented (and none from behind the Iron Curtain).

NEW YORK STATE PAVILION [43]
Philip Johnson, Richard Foster, Lev Zetlin
Flushing Meadows Park
1964, Queens

The largest, tallest, and most fun was the **NEW YORK STATE PAVILION [43]** by Philip Johnson, Richard Foster, and engineer Lev Zetlin. The pavilion's main section was the elliptical Tent of Tomorrow, which was covered by a multicolored translucent roof suspended from 100-foot columns. The Texaco New York State paper map was recreated in colorful terrazzo paving. The map captured the spirit and dynamism of the age and was one of the first large-scale pieces of public Pop Art.

Johnson commissioned several art pieces for the pavilion; the most controversial was created by friend Andy Warhol, who silk-screened portraits of the FBI's Ten Most Wanted Fugitives. Moses found it too provocative and had it painted over. At the end of the fair, the pavilion was too expensive to tear down, so it was just left to decades of neglect. Plans to refurbish the pavilion may finally be in the works.

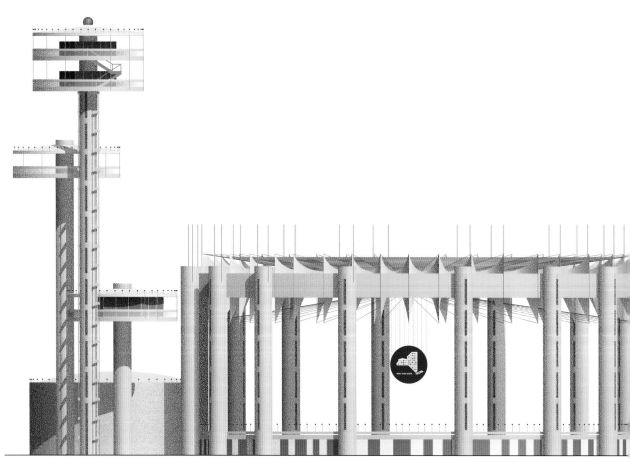

Another fair structure that still stands is the **PORT AUTHORITY BUILDING [44]** (now Terrace on the Park). It had a heliport on its roof where choppers brought fair attendees from local airports as well as Manhattan. Below the landing deck was a thousand-seat restaurant with an expansive view of Queens. The building now survives as a catering hall. The extremely popular Spanish Pavilion designed by Javier Carvajal was also preserved, but not in New York. The pavilion was moved piece by piece to St. Louis, Missouri, where it became part of a hotel. The eighty-foot Uniroyal Giant Tire Ferris wheel was also salvaged and was rolled away to Michigan.

Overall visitor numbers were low, due in part to high prices and because out-of-towners might have been frightened by the widely publicized Harlem Race Riot of 1964. Also, with the world coming closer because of air and automobile travel—not to mention the popularity of television—there might have been a feeling that fairs like these were antiquated, and the event was the last of its kind, in New York City at least. A record crowd of 446,953 showed up for the closing day, which turned into a frenzied hunt for souvenirs. Elegant ladies dug up flowers and carried them away in their hats. Everything from saltshakers to Egypt's statue of King Tut was stolen or smashed. It was a frightening end to an era.

PORT AUTHORITY BUILDING [44]
(Terrace on the Park)
Port Authority Architects
Flushing Meadows Park
1964, Queens

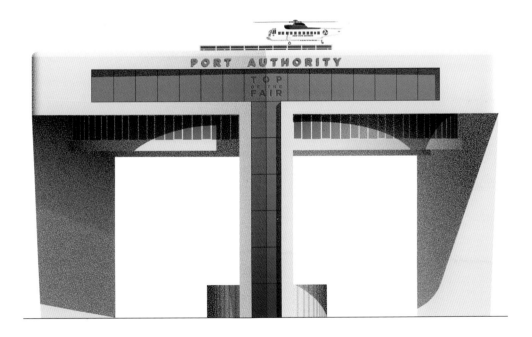

Old values seemed to crumble away, but organized religion was determined to be represented: Mormons, Christian Scientists, and even the Vatican opened their own pavilions at the World's Fair. But those were temporary structures. Cast in solid concrete, Staten Island's **ALBA HOUSE [45]** (also known as Society of St. Paul Seminary) was more permanent. Tasked with spreading the word of God, the building contained a massive printing house, including offices, bookstore, and a chapel.

Editors of the brilliant *AIA Guide To New York City* called it, "Staten Island's most bizarre building," and they are probably right. The exterior resembles a modern sculpture. The brutalist structure of concrete and glass has an expressive staircase that leads to a boldly structured roof that seemed to long for a touch from Heaven.

ALBA HOUSE [45]
(Society of St. Pauls)
Silverman & Cika
2187 Victory Blvd,
Westerleigh
1969, Staten Island

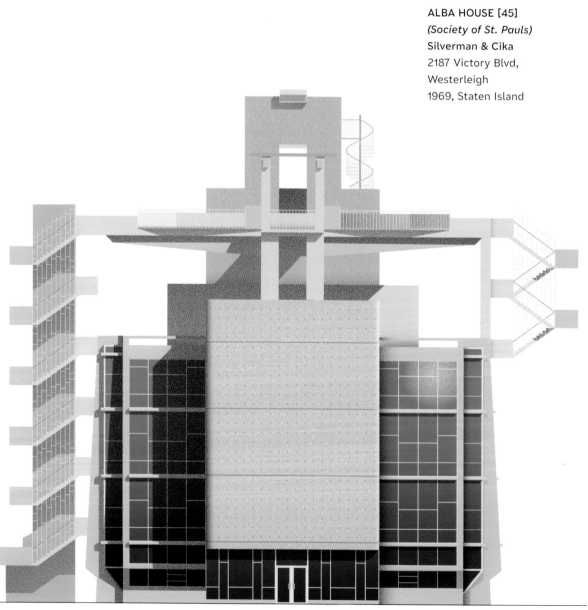

Staten Island was going through a rapid transformation. After decades of false starts, a physical link with Brooklyn was finally realized in the form of the Verrazzano-Narrows Bridge. The world's longest suspension crossing at the time, the bridge's five-year construction was touchingly chronicled in Gay Talese's *The Bridge*. As a result, land prices on Staten Island went through the roof and suburban houses became the hottest new crop on the island's fields.

As middle classes left for suburbs, their old neighborhoods became home to newcomers from the rural south and Puerto Rico (in both places, modernization of farming had resulted in mass unemployment). Landlords often profited from the change as they subdivided the old houses to squeeze in more tenants, charging higher rents. Using a technique called blockbusting to frighten people into moving out because minorities were moving in, real estate agents hired Black people to walk with baby carriages and to drive around with radios blasting. They staged street fights in white neighborhoods to scare homeowners into selling under market price.

Meanwhile, racially mixed neighborhoods in attractive locations were labeled as slums, torn down, and replaced by racially and economically segregated housing. Stores, small workshops, and other chances of local employment were transformed into empty green lawns and parking lots. Because NYCHA's projects had strict maximum income levels, once a family's financial situation improved, they had to move out. It created a perpetual loop that trapped families over generations. Accordingly, the projects concentrated less economically successful families in an area, many of which lost connections to informal networks that were needed to thrive in the city.

This was just one of many reasons for growing resistance to large-scale urban renewal projects. Local communities began to organize and fight back. Jane Jacobs became an icon of the movement for defeating Moses's plan to cut a wide road—to accommodate more car traffic, of course—through Washington Square Park in Greenwich Village. In her 1961 book *The Death and Life American Cities*, Jacobs used common sense to point out what was wrong with contemporary urban planning and offered solutions on how to design cities to be safer and more livable for everyone. The book remains influential to this day, and her name has become synonymous with community-inclusive planning.

SWIMMOBILES. In the 1960s, the city renewed construction of municipal pools, which had largely stopped after the New Deal money dried up. It was believed that the pools could keep teenagers out of trouble during the long summer days. Before permanent facilities were built, the Parks Department had five swimmobiles—forty-foot-long metal pools that were towed each day from Randall's Island to a different destination.[27]

Gradually, new housing projects became smaller and built where they would displace the least number of people, or in the case of **BRIDGE APARTMENTS [46]**, where the displacement already happened. The homes of 1,850 families were razed in the construction of the link between the George Washington Bridge and Cross Bronx Expressway. The Trans-Manhattan Expressway was a block-wide scar that cut through Washington Heights. Someone came up with the idea of building housing on top of the twelve-lane expressway.

In the 1960s architects were always working on concepts for how to include housing as part of highways and bridges. Bridge Apartments proved just how bad an idea this was. The four colossal blocks stood like a row of dominoes over traffic running into the open ditch below. Noxious fumes, dust, and constant noise made the balconies on the lower floors unusable. Tenants felt the vibrations as a constant flow of trucks passed underneath. Robert F. Kennedy, the president's brother and New York senator eyeing the presidency, visited the buildings and publicly criticized the "total disregard for environmental factors on the part of our city planners."

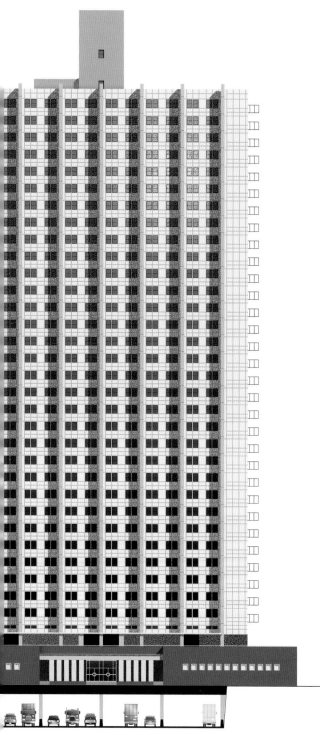

BRIDGE APARTMENTS [46]
Brown & Guenther
1365 Saint Nicholas Ave,
Washington Heights
1963, Manhattan

The project was originally built under the state's Mitchell-Lama Program for affordable moderate- and middle-income housing and provided 960 large apartments. Some 4,000 people call it home now, many of them large families. Living in the apartments improved with time: Single-glazed windows were replaced with double-glazed ones that muffled road noise better. According to interviews with the residents, they have grown used to the noise and vibrations and don't even notice it anymore.

This expressway continues into the Bronx, where it becomes the Cross Bronx Expressway. New York University's campus at University Heights (now Bronx Community College) overlooks it. The ranks of students rapidly expanded in the postwar years, and the university was busy constructing new facilities for their Science and Engineering Schools. The choice of Marcel Breuer, the Hungarian-born architect and furniture designer, was a sign of the institution's growing confidence.

Breuer designed the new buildings in uncompromising brutalist style, which contrasted outrageously with Stamford White's Classical Revival design for the rest of the campus. The most unusual of the new facilities was the trapezoidal-shaped **BEGRISCH HALL AT BRONX COMMUNITY COLLEGE [47]**. On each side of the heavy base are two stepped-up, cantilevered lecture halls. Begrisch Hall is physically separated from the laboratory building and linked via an elevated bridge. The building is faced with exposed concrete and textured with visible marks left by the formwork boards.

BEGRISCH HALL AT BRONX
COMMUNITY COLLEGE [47]
Marcel Breuer
2155 University Ave, University Heights
1961, the Bronx

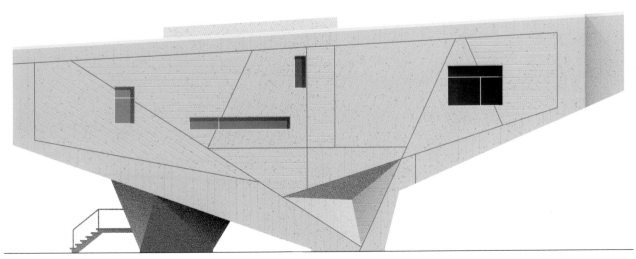

As the military draft expanded and students faced the possibility of being sent to fight in the Vietnam War, college campuses all over the country became the scene of both antiwar protests and support-our-troops parades.

While the United States sent tens of thousands of young men and billions of dollars to the jungles of southeast Asia to fight against Communism, the country also was fighting a war on the cultural home front. The construction of Lincoln Center for the Performing Arts was part of the offensive against the notion that capitalistic America was materialistic and culturally shallow. Wallace Harrison, architect of the Metropolitan Opera House at the heart of the complex, said the undertaking proved that even "we so-called monopolistic, imperialistic degenerates are capable of building the greatest cultural center in the world."

It wasn't built just for the outside world though. John D. Rockefeller III (one of Junior's sons) and other leading figures financing the center were concerned that the newly affluent society had too much free time on their hands and if not guided properly, they could fall into an existential void. It's safe to say that the families displaced during the demolition of the eighteen city blocks had more pressing concerns than boredom. The neighborhood before it was demolished, San Juan Hill, can be seen in 1961's *West Side Story*.

NEW YORK STATE THEATER [50]
(David H. Koch Theater)
Philip Johnson, John Burgee
20 Lincon Center Plaza, Lincoln Square
1964, Manhattan

METROPOLITAN OPERA HOUSE [48]
Wallace Harrison
30 Lincon Center Plaza, Lincoln Square
1966, Manhattan

Lincoln Center was formed around a Philip Johnson-designed square. The three buildings enclosing the space look remarkably similar at the first glance, as their architects agreed on a set of unifying elements. Clad in travertine from a quarry near Rome (the same stone was used to clad the Coliseum), the buildings have the identical second-floor balconies that are all the same height. Harrison was constantly badgered to become a chief architect of the Center, but he refused after the awful experience he had during the construction of the UN.

Harrison chose to design only the **METROPOLITAN OPERA HOUSE [48]**, the focal point of the plaza. Unfortunately for him, it was another traumatic experience. In a long and tortuous process, Harrison had to prepare forty-three different designs. The budget was drastically cut multiple times, compromising his vision. A gift of two dozen starburst chandeliers from the Austrian government brightened the economized interior.

Harrison brought in his office partner, Max Abramovitz, to design the **PHILHARMONIC HALL [49]** (now David Geffen Hall) next door. It was the first structure to be finished. The otherwise solid building had one important flaw however: Its concert hall had terrible acoustics. It was completely redesigned a decade later, and again in 2022. Johnson was responsible for **NEW YORK STATE THEATER [50]** (now David H. Koch Theater), which was praised for its functional and efficient layout.

Harrison's career as essentially the personal architect of the Rockefeller family ended prematurely. His lifeless extension to Rockefeller Center and imperious Empire State Plaza in Albany were severely criticized. Nelson Rockefeller, the most successful of Junior's sons and the architect's close friend, shunned him. Harrison became a bitter old man and complained that "America is the only country to pass from barbarism to degeneration without passing through civilization." But his rags-to-riches career said otherwise.

PHILHARMONIC HALL [49]
(David Geffen Hall)
Max Abramovitz
10 Lincoln Center Plaza, Lincoln Square
1962, Manhattan

Way up in the northeast part of the Bronx rose **CO-OP CITY [51]**, the largest such development in the world. It was built on swampy land that had been the site of the defunct Freedomland U.S.A. amusement park. Co-Op City's towers (and a few row houses) contained an incredible 15,372 apartments, housing more than 55,000 people.

"Almost single-handedly, Co-Op City appeared to drain the lifeblood from the Grand Concourse," wrote Constance Rosenblum, pointing out how the population of formerly thriving Bronx boulevard left en masse for the new development. The early tenants were overwhelmingly Jewish families seeking a safer and more comfortable place to live. Crime in the borough was already on the rise in the old neighborhoods and reports of violence in newspapers and on television news shows accelerated the exit of people to Co-Op City.

CO-OP CITY [51]
Herman Jessor
140 Alcott Pl, Co-Op City
1967-1973, the Bronx

94

The design of **MACY'S [52]** (now Queens Place Mall) in Elmhurst, Queens, was a result of several limitations of its site. The circular plan was deemed the best fit for the irregularly shaped plot and the site's high water table didn't allow for underground garages, so the architects wrapped five rings of parking spaces around the mall. To avoid the need for mechanical ventilation and allow fumes to escape, the facade was designed as a grill. Two one-way helix ramps led cars on and off the five levels and a super-modern computerized signal system was installed to show drivers the location of available parking spots.

But there was one snag in all this: One homeowner refused to sell. After refusing offers five times the market value for her corner-site house, Macy's capitulated. The architects had to cut a little notch into the building's otherwise perfect circular plan. In all, the building was considerably more costly than the traditional suburban malls that were springing up around the city's fringes, but the extra investment was worth it since the area had relatively high population density and LeFrak City was fairly close by.

NEW YORK CITY SMOG, 1966. The annual Macy's Thanksgiving Day Parade got a dark twist in 1966. Pollution from traffic, garbage incinerators, and factories got trapped over New York because of inversion weather, creating toxic smog conditions. The heavy smog was more than evident to the one million people watching the parade. The city declared a smog alert and for three days the city was enshrouded in a toxic fugue. In the end, the death toll totaled more than two hundred people. The outcry over poor air quality in the city and across the country led to the introduction of the Clean Air Act, which improved air quality nationwide.[28]

MACY'S [52] *(Queens Place Mall, Stern's)*
Skidmore Owings & Merrill
88-01 Queens Boulevard, Elmhurst
1965, Queens

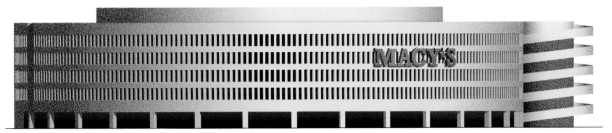

1970s

Ungovernable and broke, New York had reached rock bottom in the 1970s. The Fun City of the 1960s became Fear City. Ivy League Mayor Lindsay wasn't fresh anymore and was replaced by London-born Abe Beame, an accountant educated in the city's public school system. The city's financial woes weren't the only trouble. In July 1977, a massive power failure caused a blackout, plunging the city streets into darkness. Looters ransacked stores and arsonists set the city on fire. Some 1,600 shops were damaged and many of them wouldn't reopen. As if that wasn't enough, a crazed serial killer known as Son of Sam began terrorizing the city.

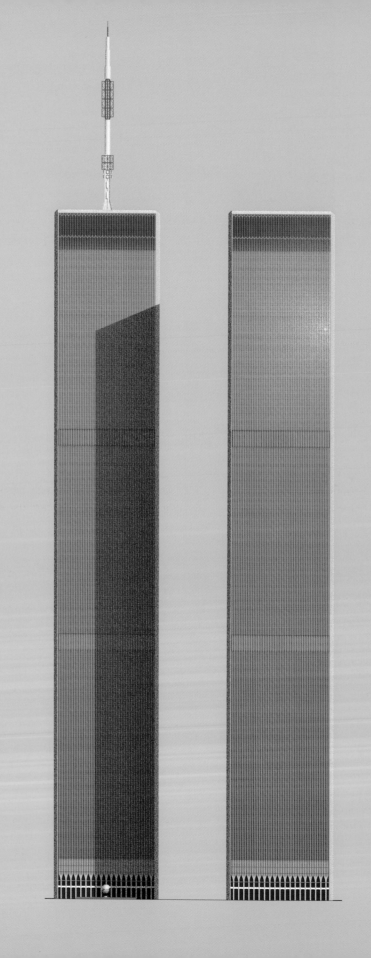

The Port Authority of New York and New Jersey had an unusual problem—it had too much money. Tolls on its bridges and tunnels brought in so much profit that pressure grew on the agency to pour some of the profit into the ailing mass-transit system. But conversely, a well-invested subway takes away cars from the roads, leading to less toll revenue. To avoid this, the money was pumped into financing construction of the **WORLD TRADE CENTER [53]** (1 WTC and 2 WTC, or the Twin Towers) development initiated by David Rockefeller. The project was obviously out of the Port Authority's mandate, which was supposed to focus on infrastructure, but officials reasoned the offices would house import-export companies operating from the port.

The office building mania of the 1960s happened mostly in Midtown while downtown's Financial District was flagging. Some powerful companies and individuals, like the Rockefellers, owned land in the area and keenly backed any project to keep the land prices high. Minoru Yamasaki was chosen as the architect of the WTC. Born in Seattle to Japanese immigrants, Yamasaki spent five grueling summers in Alaska working at a fish cannery to pay for his college. But despite the hard scrabble years, Yamasaki's work was known for delicate details and patterns. However, it wasn't considered fashionable at the time, and some critics dismissed him as a merely a "decorator."

Despite designing the tallest buildings in the world, Yamasaki had a fear of heights and had never drawn plans for a skyscraper before. But he turned that into an advantage and together with his partners, Emery Roth & Sons,

WORLD TRADE CENTER [53]
(1 WTC & 2 WTC, or the Twin Towers)
Minoru Yamasaki, Emery Roth & Sons
World Trade Center,
Financial District
1973-2001, Manhattan

introduced many ingenious solutions. Unusually, he came up with a facade that was load bearing, thus removing the need for interior columns and creating a huge open space. As a result the windows were so narrow that people could rest their shoulders on the chunky pillars framing them, and so reducing vertigo. Innovative floor trusses made floors much thinner and allowed more stories to be packed into the building.

SUBWAY REDESIGN. Until consolidation in 1940, the New York subway system was operated by three different private companies. The stations, however, remained a chaotic mix of the different styles, and navigating through the system was tough. Italian designer Massimo Vignelli visually unified all the stations and lines with new minimalist signage that won him universal acclaim. Despite this success, his radically simplified subway map, similar to that of the London Tube map, never won the heart of New Yorkers and was replaced just seven years later.

As a government agency, the Port Authority was exempt from the city's fire codes. But after the 1974 release of *The Towering Inferno*, a film about a vertiginous skyscraper that goes up in flames because the builder had cut corners in construction, critics decried the lack of fire sprinklers in the towers. One of the reasons so many new construction solutions were used was that the Port Authority was a government agency and didn't necessarily have to bother about the city building code. Instead of traditional solutions like fireproof bricks, which protected the steel frame if the Empire State Building in the 1945 plane crash, the Port Authority used a brand-new spray-on insulation that was lightweight and thin. This opened up more floor space but offered little protection in a case of a blast or impact.

Meanwhile, Yamasaki struggled with the style of the towers. He later described how his daughter, upon seeing one of the early, decorative models, criticized it. That was his breaking point: He would go against his intuition and design a building he thought his critics would like, something more minimalist and severe. But the new designs were just as harshly criticized, with one comment saying they were "the boxes that the Empire State Building and the Chrysler Building came in." (In an ironic twist, the ape in the 1976 remake of *King Kong* climbed up the Twin Towers instead of the Empire State Building.) Eventually, New Yorkers came to love the towers, affectionately dubbing them the Twin Towers, and they were greatly mourned after the horrific attacks of September 11, 2001, completely destroyed them.

Harlem was in a long-sustained decline. Most of the Black middle class had relocated to the few suburbs that allowed non-white homeownership. Conrad Johnson remembered better days. He grew up in the city during the Harlem Renaissance, the great revival of African American arts and politics, and his dad was a respected politician.

SIKORSKI S-61S CRASH. The helipad on top of the PanAm Building was always controversial because of the noise generated by the helicopters in an area full of buildings where people were trying to work. To speed up the boarding process, the helicopters loaded and unloaded the passengers with the rotors running. One day, the landing gear snapped and the helicopter tilted over and killed four people waiting to board. The broken-off blade then sailed down to the street and killed a pedestrian. The city immediately revoked New York Airlines's permit and the dream was over.

When the Second World War came, Johnson served as a pilot in the legendary Tuskegee Airmen unit and returned home a hero. He wanted to continue flying as a commercial pilot, but no airline would employ him. So he went on to study architecture instead. His first commission was a house for his parents in a suburb away from Harlem.

Johnson was running an architecture company with Percy Ifill, his childhood friend and fellow Harlemite. Governor Nelson Rockefeller commissioned them to design a new government building on 125th Street, Harlem's most important thoroughfare. The **HARLEM STATE OFFICE BUILDING [54]**, a big office tower with a public plaza that required half a city block of homes and businesses to be torn down, wasn't exactly what anyone wanted in this neighborhood. The nineteen-story brutalist box became known under the technically correct acronym SOB. Of it, *New York Times* architecture critic Paul Goldberger said, "If nothing else, this proves that the State of New York is evenhanded—it is willing to give Harlem the same mediocre architecture it dishes out everywhere else."

Home to a fast-growing Puerto Rican (as well as Dominican and Mexican) community, East Harlem became known as Spanish Harlem, or El Barrio. There had been a lot of slum clearance in the last two decades that had uprooted existing neighborhoods, and the area now had the highest concentration of public housing in the whole city.[29] Most of the projects were towers or slabs devoid of any traces of the communities and businesses that were once here.

HARLEM STATE OFFICE BUILDING [54] *(Adam Clayton Powell, Jr. State Office Building)*
Ifill Johnson Hanchard
163 W 125th St, Harlem
1973, Manhattan

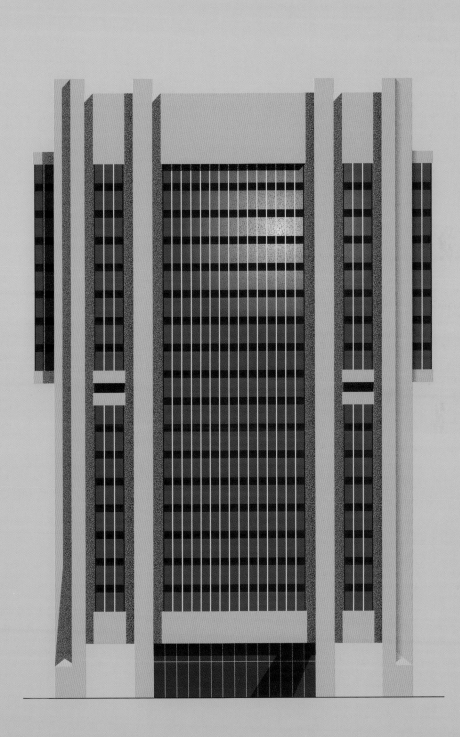

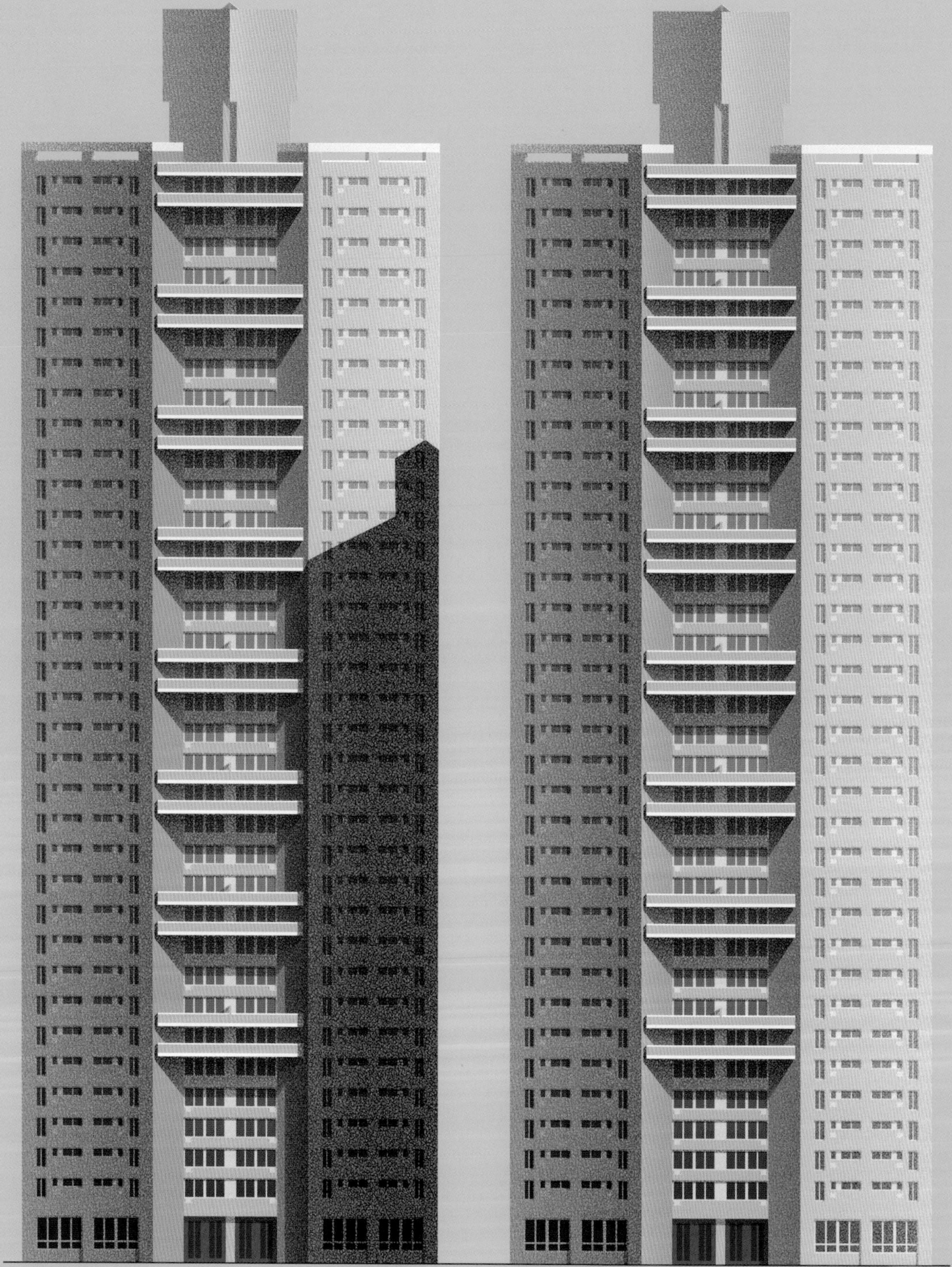

SCHOMBURG PLAZA [55] was set to be different—a new kind of development that would mix people of all races and incomes. It was proposed by Mamie Phipps Clark and Kenneth B. Clark, two pioneering Black psychologists. It was set to have an equal mix of Black, Hispanic, and white residents, but things didn't go as planned. The site, at the northeast corner of Central Park, happened to be the headquarters of the New York Young Lords. This organization, inspired by the Black Panthers, campaigned for better access to healthcare, services, and housing for Latinos.

The Young Lords pressed for bigger inclusion of Hispanic contractors and tenants. And when advertising in mainstream newspapers brought very little interest from white families, the project became a fifty-fifty mix of Black and Hispanic tenants.[30] There were 600 units spread in the two octagonal towers and one slab, as well as a day care center and commercial space.

Families from the area, especially those displaced by the slum clearance, got first dibs. The development was aptly named for Arturo Alfonso Schomburg, a Black Puerto Rican writer and collector of African art (Schomburg Center for Research in Black Culture is also located in Harlem). Much later, in 2005, the project was bought out of the Mitchell-Lama Program and rechristened with the meaningless name, The Heritage.

Inflation caused by the Vietnam War was made worse by the oil embargo, a reaction by oil-producing Arab nations to the US support of Israel. The economy suffered and jobs disappeared. The crisis in the inner cities, brewing for decades, started to take center stage in American minds. Contemporary newspapers and TV made this brewing crisis look like an almost exclusively New York City affair. The city was the scene of some of the worst excesses, but far from unique as other cities across the nation faced similar issues.

The news, both in print and on television nightly, pushed the narrative of violence and increasing urban decay in the city. Suburbanites were subject to constant negative coverage as the evening news featured reports set in the ruins of the Bronx, and the newspapers hammered on about the city's supposedly misguided generosity toward the lower classes. This perceived downturn in addition to the city being on the brink of bankruptcy brought little sympathy from the rest of the country. Even President Ford, quoted on front pages as having told the city to "Drop Dead," was initially against providing any help.

The fiscal crisis wasn't a product of the 1970s, but rather the conclusion of decades of financial mismanagement, corruption, and short-sightedness. The city's tax base was shrinking as its expenses were rising dramatically. The city was deeply in debt and to keep making payments on existing loans, it borrowed more and more each month.

SCHOMBURG PLAZA [55]
(The Heritage)
Gruzen & Partners; Castro-Blanco, Piscioneri & Feder
1295 5th Ave, East Harlem
1975, Manhattan

When banks refused to lend the city more money and the city inched toward bankruptcy, a deal was made: Control of the city was handed to a group representing the creditors, largely unelected "representatives" who reported to the investors and not the city's residents. The group fired sixty thousand city workers, salaries were frozen, taxes increased, and services like health care, police, and fire were drastically cut. Firing thousands of cops amidst the skyrocketing crime spree made little sense to anyone—except the city's creditors.

During this time, the NYPD headquarters was moved from the opulent 240 Center Street, its home for sixty-four years, to the modern **ONE POLICE PLAZA [56]**. The new building, sitting at the base of the Brooklyn Bridge, was linked to the Civic Center with a pedestrian bridge so wide it created a plaza of its own. Out of the windowless base that housed a shooting range and garage rose a brick cube with offices, a communication center, and a 1,200-person auditorium. It was designed by Gruzen & Partners, a firm that was responsible for practically every new building around city hall.

ONE POLICE PLAZA [56]
Gruzen & Partners
1 Police Plaza Path,
Civic District
1973, Manhattan

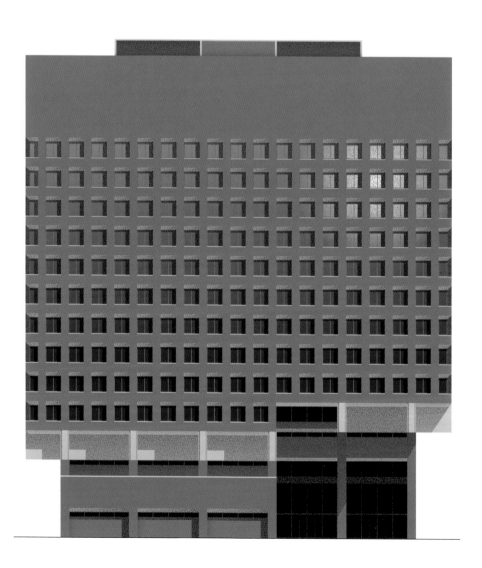

A couple of blocks away rose **33 THOMAS STREET [57]** (originally AT&T Long Lines Building). San Francisco–based John Carl Warnecke did his best to design the windowless skyscraper as agreeably as possible. He skillfully sculpted the massive fifty-story building, placing the focus on the giant air vents. The communications machines living inside didn't need a view but a supply of air to cool them down.

Over time, as the machines got smaller, the space was filled with computer servers. The building now contains a data center and, reportedly, is a hub of the National Security Agency (NSA). The ultra-secure building was clad in fireproof Swedish granite and supposedly able to withstand a nuclear blast and operate self-sufficiently—it has its own generators, fuel, food, and water supply— for up to 1,500 people for two weeks.

Movies and novels about the Cold War were still popular, and the destruction of the Big Apple often uncomfortably figured in them. In *Fail-Safe* (1963), the United States accidentally sends bombers to drop a nuke on Moscow. The President's solution? Nuke New York too, supposedly to prevent WWIII and show compassion to the Soviets.

A new crop of movies like *Death Wish* (1974) and *Taxi Driver* (1976) portrayed New York City as overrun by crazed murderers. But probably one of the most realistic depictions of the city at that time was the black comedy *The Out-of-Towners* (1970). In the movie, Jack Lemmon's character comes to town from Ohio for a big job interview, but he soon finds himself immersed in both a transit and sanitation strike and gets mugged for his wallet and watch in Central Park.

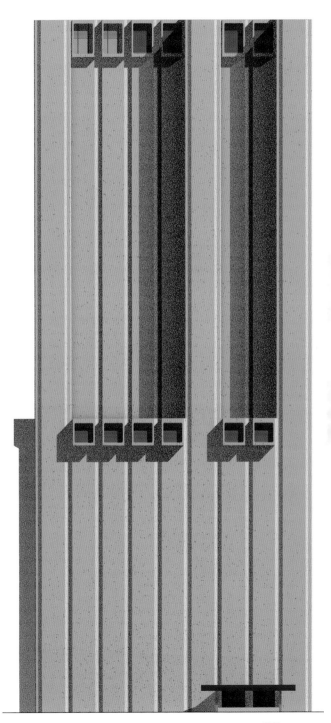

33 THOMAS STREET [57]
(AT&T Long Lines Building)
John Carl Warnecke
33 Thomas St, Tribeca
1974, Manhattan

Movies like these, while somewhat accurate portrayals of the city at the time, weren't helping its reputation around the world. As the city's economy was crashing, demand for office space also fell. Corporations began to leave the city for the suburbs or different states altogether. This meant that new construction also took a downturn.

CITIGROUP CENTER [58] (originally Citycorp Center) was the only large office building completed in all of 1977. As the developers purchased the smaller lots to make the whole, they stumbled upon a problem: A small church wouldn't sell. A charismatic local priest urged his flock to resist the buyout and stay put. The financial corporation, unable to move them, built the shell of a new, modern chapel building on the corner and paid a sizable "donation" for the trouble. This exercise reportedly made the assembled site the most expensive in the world.

Massachusetts-based architect Hugh Stubbins designed the skyscraper with cantilevered corners to allow space for the new church structure. He added a ski-slope roof that made the building instantly recognizable. The construction also included The Market, a three-level mall of shops and restaurants, entrance to St. Peter's Church, as well as expanded connection to various subway lines beneath the tower.

The skyscraper was structurally challenging, given the height—at the time it was seventh tallest in the world—and the unusual cantilevered corners and angled roof. It was the first skyscraper in New York to feature a tuned mass damper to limit the sway caused by winds, essentially a huge block of concrete sitting in a pool of oil under the roof that counteracts the swaying motion.

A year after Citigroup Center opened, Diane Hartley, an undergraduate student at Princeton University, was writing a thesis on the building. She found discrepancies in the structural calculations and contacted the firm responsible for the skyscraper's engineering. The firm assured her everything was correct, and she let the matter go.

Some twenty years later Hartley found out that her inquiry led the chief engineer to discover dangerous structural issues—issues caused by cost-cutting changes made by the steel supplier. This spurred a secret repair operation. Pressed on by a coming superstorm, teams of welders snuck into the building under cover of the night to fix it. Only a handful of people were aware of the operation.

NYPD PLYMOUTH FURY. In an attempt to make the police look more accessible and friendly, cars were replaced with light-blue-and-white models instead of dark green and black. Police uniforms were also changed to light blue as well, which proved unwise as they made stains and sweat more visible. (The color of the nightsticks remained the same.)

CITIGROUP CENTER [58]
(Citycorp Center)
Hugh Stubbins, Emery Roth & Sons
153 East 53rd Street, Midtown
1977, Manhattan

SANITATION SERVICES. Budget cuts hit every city service, no matter how essential. And when cuts were demanded from the Department of Sanitation (DSNY), New York became notably dirtier. The DSNY had to cut the frequency of garbage collection and street cleaning everywhere—most notably in depopulating areas of the outer boroughs.

With all the problems the city had had with urban renewal projects, the focus was now on developing sites that didn't require dislocating residents. **TRACEY TOWERS [59]** were built over Jerome subway yard in the Bronx. Tracey Towers were designed by Kentucky-born Paul Rudolph, the country's most notable brutalist architect. The developer asked Rudolph to design a circular building, but Rudolph wanted to avoid the oval-shaped rooms because they are difficult to furnish.

Rudolph came up with curved vertical elements projecting from the building that make the building appear round. This design also somewhat muffled the noise from the Mosholu Parkway below. The only downside is that these elements made the apartments relatively dark. Rudolph wanted the buildings to be faced with poured concrete, but budget restraints forced him to use concrete cladding instead. For three years, the towers held the title as the tallest buildings in the Bronx.

TRACEY TOWERS [59]
Paul Rudolph
40 W Mosholu Pkwy S, Jerome Park
1974, the Bronx

TRACEY TOWERS

It was **HARLEM RIVER PARK TOWERS [60]** (now River Park Residences) that stole that title from Tracey Towers. They were built on a similarly isolated site in Morris Heights bounded by the Harlem River from the west and a train line and the Major Deegan Expressway from the east. Two bridges connected the towers with the rest of the Bronx, but residents didn't necessarily need to leave the area as a school, shops, and community facilities were built on-site.

The best way to appreciate the size of the project is to see it from the Harlem River Greenway across the water. The scale is colossal: Two slabs (each a merger of a pair of towers) rise thirty-eight and forty-two stories and contain 1,654 apartments. With so many residents, elevators were a major problem. There are not enough even when they are all in service (which is not often).

The project's architects, Davis, Brody & Associates, designed oversize square "super bricks" that became their trademark. Thanks to the size, workers could build a larger area of a wall per day than with smaller bricks. The towers would grow wider toward the top, offering great views of the city. The architects had used the same style and materials on Waterside Plaza on the East River, which had opened the year before.

HARLEM RIVER PARK TOWERS [60]
(Richman Plaza / River Park Residences)
Davis, Brody & Associates
20 Richman Plaza, Morris Heights
1975, the Bronx

Roosevelt Island (once named Blackwell's Island) was nicknamed "Welfare Island" because it once served as a convenient depository of the old, poor, and mentally challenged. Plans were now in the works to develop this island in the East River into a brand-new community for people of all ages and (dis)abilities. The effort was led by Ed Logue, a masterful developer of municipal projects, who cut his teeth in New Haven and Boston. **THE LANDINGS [61]** (originally Eastwood) was one of the first structures to be built.

As with other buildings on the island, The Landings was experimental in many ways. For example, hallways were shared by three stories of apartments (the units above and below had individual staircases inside) to allow residents to mingle more. A large portion of the one thousand units were reserved for people with disabilities and the elderly. But like elsewhere, money became scarce and cuts had to be made. Apartments for people with disabilities were downsized, air conditioning was axed, and the heating system was replaced with electric baseboards, which were cheaper to install but more expensive to run (about half of a building's running costs now are for energy).

The building stepped up from the river, with the tallest part facing Main Street, a shopping street that acts as a spine of the island. It was planned by Philip Johnson in what he called "his Jane Jacobs period." While the island is connected to Queens by bridge, car traffic is kept at a minimum: Residents can park their cars at the large communal garage but must walk or use the free electric bus to get around.

ROOSEVELT ISLAND TRAM. Because establishing a subway train to connect Roosevelt Island with Manhattan was consistently delayed (by thirteen years), an ingenious solution was found—an aerial tram. Designed by the engineering firm of Lev Zetlin (also responsible for New York State Pavilion) and built by a Swiss company, the tram was the world's first mass-transit tramway. It has been featured prominently in Nighthawks *(1981) and* Spiderman *(2002).*

THE LANDINGS [61]
(Eastwood)
Sert Jackson Associates
510 Main St, Roosevelt Island
1976, Manhattan

One of the projects that was heavily affected by lack of money was **WOODHULL MEDICAL AND MENTAL HEALTH CENTER [62]** in Brooklyn. It was built on the borders of three communities—Williamsburg, Bushwick, and Bedford-Stuyvesant. Designed in the radical 1960s, the structure had many innovative ideas baked in. For example, the ceilings were hollow and so thick that workers could walk inside to maintain the complex system of pipes and tubes without disrupting patients and doctors below. The column-free interior offered absolute flexibility: Everything was built in a modular fashion, so the building could be easily extended with new floors.

During the process, however, the budget climbed by 250 percent because of inflation and its unorthodox design. By the time the structure was ready to be fitted out, the city was penniless and couldn't afford to actually open and run the hospital. They approached the Justice Department and offered to sell them the building for use as a prison.[31]

It was obviously not a great idea if only because the hollow ceilings would make convenient escape routes for inmates. In the end the hospital stood empty for five years. When the city's finances improved, the hospital finally opened in 1982. By the 1980s, ideas about health care changed and the 700-foot-long dark slab clad in rust-colored corten steel was the polar opposite of the smaller, friendlier approach the hospitals were now taking. Writing about it in the *New York Times*, architecture critic Paul Goldberger perfectly described the shadowy giant as looking like "a cross between a 1920's factory and the Centre Pompidou in Paris."[32]

WOODHULL MEDICAL AND MENTAL HEALTH CENTER [62]
Kallmann & McKinnell
760 Broadway, Bedford-Stuyvesant
1977, Brooklyn

The Verrazzano-Narrows Bridge connecting Brooklyn to Staten Island proved to be extremely successful and a second deck was added just a few years after completion to cope with the increased traffic. The bridge was slightly damaged in 1973 when the aptly named ship *Sea Witch* rammed into an oil tanker leading to a huge fire. The flames were so high, they licked the bottom of the bridge and fried some equipment. The bridge was showcased in 1977's *Saturday Night Fever*.

In August 1977, notorious serial murderer David Berkowitz, aka Son of Sam, was finally apprehended by police who were able to track him because of a parking ticket. Some people morbidly joked that "in New York you can get away with murder, as long as you don't park at the fire hydrant."

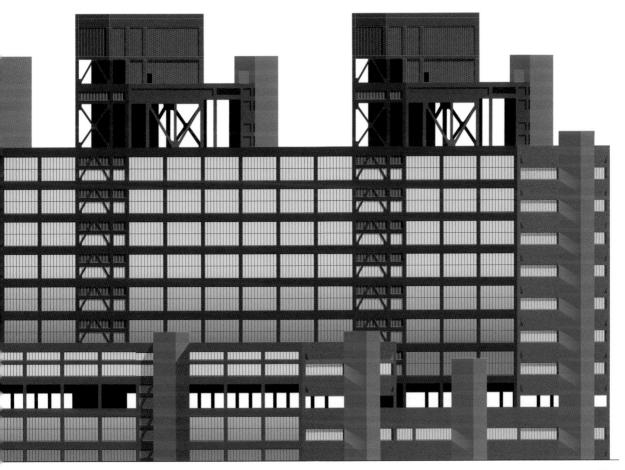

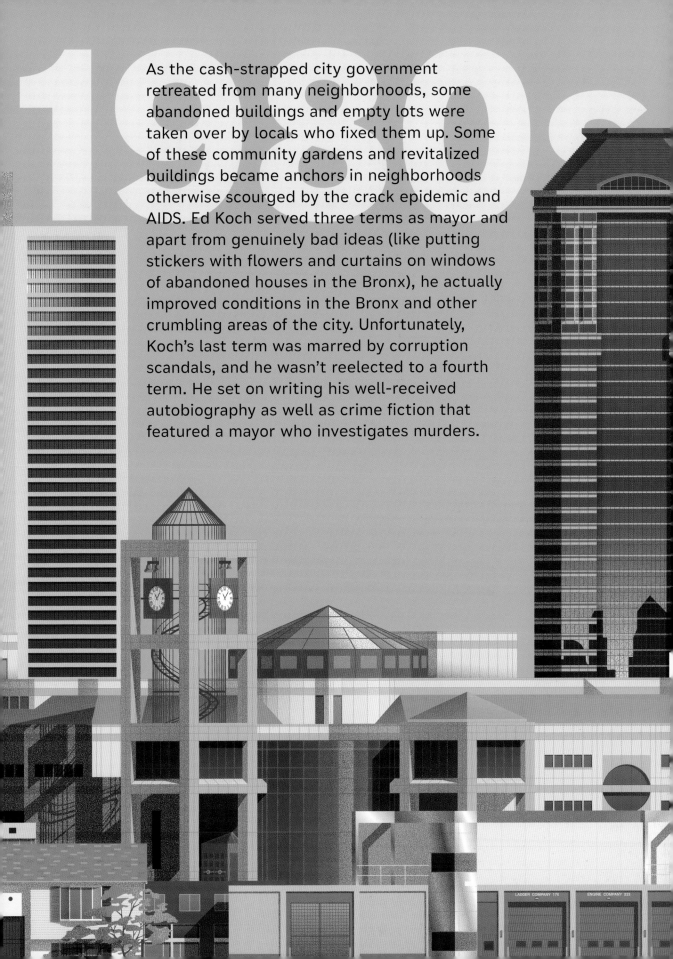

1980s

As the cash-strapped city government retreated from many neighborhoods, some abandoned buildings and empty lots were taken over by locals who fixed them up. Some of these community gardens and revitalized buildings became anchors in neighborhoods otherwise scourged by the crack epidemic and AIDS. Ed Koch served three terms as mayor and apart from genuinely bad ideas (like putting stickers with flowers and curtains on windows of abandoned houses in the Bronx), he actually improved conditions in the Bronx and other crumbling areas of the city. Unfortunately, Koch's last term was marred by corruption scandals, and he wasn't reelected to a fourth term. He set on writing his well-received autobiography as well as crime fiction that featured a mayor who investigates murders.

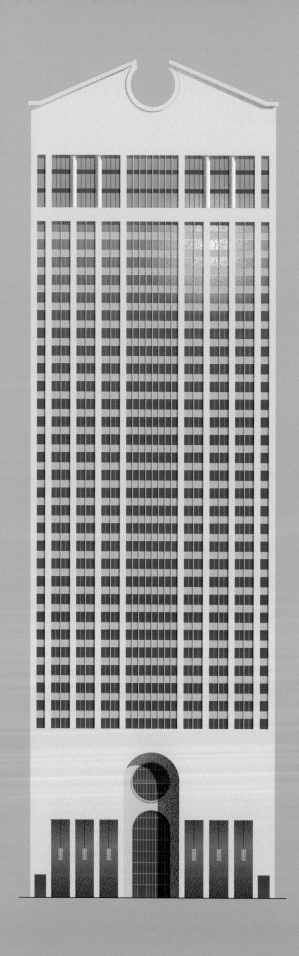

The 1980s started with cautious optimism for some. Construction cranes started to swing around town again, and new jobs appeared. The city led by Mayor Edward I. Koch was going through a fundamental shift in its policies. Brutal cuts in everything from health care to infrastructure upkeep were in contrast with generous tax breaks and other incentives corporations received. The policy shifted from social welfare to corporate welfare.

Since the late 1960s, companies were deserting Manhattan in droves, but now the tide was seeming to change. Corporate giants like IBM and AT&T built new headquarters in east Midtown. **550 MADISON AVENUE [63]** (originally AT&T Building, later Sony Tower) was the most talked about new building in New York and probably the whole country.

Architect Philip Johnson gradually progressed from minimalist modernism to what became known as postmodernism. As with any new style, postmodernism ruffled feathers of the traditionalists; it offered architects freedom to reference anything in architecture history and to use any material. Of course, only a lucky few talented architects had clients enlightened enough with budgets to fully exploit the new possibilities, so many ended up repeating newly established clichés.

Questions surrounding architecture styles usually took place in the underworld of architecture writing, but it was different this time. Johnson appeared on the cover of *Time* magazine (the last time an architect was on the cover), clutching a model of the new building. The article's message was clear from the opening sentence: "Modernism is dead."

The most upsetting part of Johnson's building was the split pediment on the roof, which made the skyscraper look like a Chippendale cabinet or a grandfather clock. But it was the less controversial elements that set the trend and were more widely accepted—stone cladding instead of glass and a public lobby in place of a plaza.

PEUGEOT TAXIS. The very first taxis used in New York City in the 1900s were built in France. Eighty years later, French cars were back in vogue because high oil prices made their fuel-efficient engines more attractive and cost-effective. But the city's bumpy, potholed roads proved unkind to delicate European-made cars. Also, in some cases, American-size customers weren't compatible with European-size backseats, so it was au revoir yet again.

550 MADISON AVENUE [63]
(AT&T Building, Sony Tower)
Philip Johnson, John Burgee
550 Madison Avenue, Financial District
1984, Manhattan

On Fifth Avenue, one block north, rose **TRUMP TOWER [64]**. Donald J. Trump was the son of Fred Trump, a developer from Queens. The younger Trump became known as "The Donald," after a journalist overheard his Czech wife, Ivana, call him that. The tower, a monument to himself, was given bonus floorspace despite not fulfilling the requirements, considerable zoning concessions by the city, and a huge tax break.

Der Scutt, the tower's architect, told neighbors complaining about the excessive shadow: "If you want sunlight, move to Kansas." The main floor housed a gaudy mall, café, and a large waterfall. These and its now infamous brass-clad escalators were listed as public amenities.

The Donald's attempts to project ego through architecture was superbly parodied in *Gremlins 2: The New Batch* (1990). His three-floor apartment at the top of the tower looked like it was decorated by a bunch of gremlins with a bucket of gold paint. After all, Steven Spielberg, the executive producer of the first *Gremlins* (1984), moved into the building too. Saudi royals and a deposed Haitian dictator lived next door.[33]

But it would be unfair to think that Trump stood out in taking advantage of the struggling city. Ayn Rand's novels promoted her philosophy of selfishness and greed as virtues and hugely influenced contemporary businesspeople and policymakers. Alan Greenspan, who steered US economic policies for twenty years, was a keen follower of her ideas. It was a time of trickle-down economics, when making the rich richer would supposedly help everyone else.

But the new age also provided new kinds of jobs on Wall Street. Between 1977 and 1984 the number of stockbrokers and dealers nearly doubled to almost 100,000. Never before could young men make so much money so quickly, and an upwardly mobile working class began to break into the world of elite banking formerly dominated by Ivy Leaguers. The risks were high, oversight was minimal, and illegal insider trading was widespread. Well-paying jobs brought an army of yuppies—young urban professionals—back to the city from the suburbs their parents had fled to decades earlier.

AIDS. When the mysterious illness first appeared, it was thought to only affect gay men and so was largely ignored by politicians. The gay community fought a long, hard battle to get needed help, but the response was painfully slow. In 1987, AIDS was the leading cause of death for New Yorkers under forty.[34]

TRUMP TOWER [64]
Der Scutt
721 Fifth Avenue, Midtown
1983, Manhattan

J.P. Morgan was one of the biggest names on Wall Street. The bank threatened to move to Delaware, but Mayor Koch successfully plied them with generous incentives to stay. **60 WALL STREET [65]** (originally J.P. Morgan Bank Building) was the first major postmodern building to grace the Financial District. The building, designed by Kevin Roche and John Dinkeloo, was a scaled-up reinterpretation of a classic column with all its elements.

The neighboring 55 Wall Street, dating back to 1842, provided not only inspiration for the building's arcaded lobby, but also its unused air rights. As a tool to tame redevelopment pressure in certain areas, a code was introduced in the 1960s that allowed selling an existing building's permitted, yet unutilized, air rights to neighboring sites. The building's considerable bulk was still beyond the ordinary limitations, as were 550 Madison Avenue and Trump Tower, and it was a result of growingly "flexible" planning policy.

It was a time of frantic men in striped suits clutching brick-size cell phones and women in blouses and jackets with oversize shoulder pads and hairdos to match. The mood was immortalized in Tom Wolfe's novel *The Bonfire of the Vanities* (1987) and movies like *Wall Street* (1985) and *Working Girl* (1988). The latter's hero is an ambitious woman working on Wall Street, commuting daily on the ferry from Staten Island.

Commuting on the Staten Island Ferry was convenient in real life as well. And as the underfunded subway became slower, dirtier, and more dangerous, the breezy twenty-five minutes on the ferry was an attractive option. Catering to the needs of the Manhattan refugees, two old warehouses, a short walk away from the St. George terminal, were converted into trendy loft apartments.

INTREPID SEA, AIR, & SPACE MUSEUM. The museum, featuring the decommissioned aircraft carrier USS Intrepid, *opened its watertight doors to visitors in 1982. Docked on Pier 86 in Hell's Kitchen, the museum's collection of historic US Navy aircraft (including the diesel-powered* Growler *submarine) was expanded with superstars of the aviation world like the Concorde, Lockheed A-12 (a military spy plane), and even the space shuttle* Enterprise.

60 WALL STREET [65]
(J.P. Morgan Bank Building)
Roche-Dinkeloo
60 Wall St, Financial District
1989, Manhattan

The six- and seven-story warehouses, built between the 1880s and 1920s, had been sitting abandoned for years before someone realized that storing yuppies, instead of sacks of coffee, was the way forward. The promotional brochure for the **BAY STREET LANDING [66]** contained a cryptic message: "Enjoy the city—the very best possible way—from your home across the Bay."

But not everyone wanted to live in the sleepy (and safe) St. George area. Since the late 1960s, middle-class folk, priced out of Manhattan and with disdain of suburbia, were instead flocking to parts of Brooklyn. Lawyers, architects, and artists bought and fixed up brownstones in places like Park Slope and Cobble Hill, reversing the process of decay still seen across other parts the borough. But this wasn't the case in other parts of Brooklyn like Ocean Hill, located between Brownsville and Bedford-Stuyvesant.

BAY STREET LANDING [66]
David Kenneth Specter & Associates
80 Bay Street Landing, St. George
1987, Staten Island

Divestment followed the "white flight," and many of the houses and local shops were abandoned or destroyed by arson during the 1977 blackout. The neighborhood was a shadow of its former self. Construction of **FIREHOUSE FOR ENGINE COMPANY 233 AND LADDER COMPANY 176 [67]** was a tentative sign that the city might finally begin reinvesting in deprived neighborhoods.

This wasn't just any firehouse: It was designed by Peter Eisenman, a prominent champion of deconstructivism that along with postmodernism evolved from the modernism movement. Today Eisenman is best known for his hauntingly powerful Holocaust Memorial in Berlin. The firehouse is located near Broadway's elevated rail tracks and references them in an exposed structural frame. Clad in stainless steel, the frame sticks out at the second floor and is aligned with the tracks at a 45-degree angle to the rest of the building.

LIME YELLOW FIRE TRUCK. Based in the South Bronx, Engine 73 was one of eleven trucks experimentally painted in a lime-yellow color because research found that the color was more visible than red and that yellow trucks got into fewer accidents. Firefighters, however, reported that people kept calling their trucks ugly. One firefighter commented with a deliberate double meaning: "We just don't want to be called yellow."

FIREHOUSE FOR ENGINE COMPANY 233 AND LADDER COMPANY 176 [67]
Peter Eisenman
25 Rockaway Ave, Ocean Hill
1985, Brooklyn

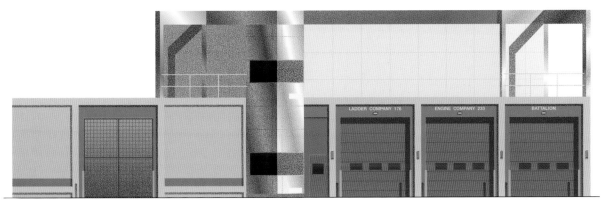

The South Bronx was a part of the city most damaged by fires at the time. There were multiple reasons behind this. Landlords, unable to find tenants or buyers, set fire to their own buildings to collect insurance payouts. Some were accidents, as electric wiring overloaded when residents used ovens and cookers to heat up apartments that lacked working radiators. Still others were torched by scrap collectors. It was so bad that tenants slept fully clothed with their shoes by the bed, ready to bolt outside if they smelled smoke. Locks and latches on doors and fire escapes that were supposed to keep burglars out often proved a fatal barrier when there was a fire.

City services like garbage collection were also cut or stopped completely. From the 1960s to 1980s, the cityscape gradually turned into a moonscape. A German film crew making a documentary about the firebombing of Dresden actually came to the city to get some stock footage.

The formerly tree-lined Charlotte Street in the South Bronx was one of the worst examples of this landlord-prompted arson trend. The remains were so "photogenic" that they attracted both presidents Jimmy Carter and Ronald Reagan. Carter called it "the worst slum in America." The Mid-Bronx Desperadoes, a local community group, fought for funds to revive the area. One member, Genevieve Brooks, originally from South Carolina, worked with urban planner Ed Logue on an unorthodox scheme for rebuilding.

CHARLOTTE GARDENS [68]
Charlotte St, Charlotte Gardens
1980s, the Bronx

CHARLOTTE GARDENS [68] was a change of pace for Logue, who was used to working with big budgets and a top-down approach. The funding for this project was uncertain, and it was being developed in close cooperation with the community. The locals wanted what the suburbanites had—to own a house with a patch of land and, as homeowners, to have a stake in improving the area. It seemed contrary to prevailing thought to build in such low density in the middle of an urbanized borough, but the times demanded new solutions.

Under the watch of a local gang hired as security, some ninety prefabricated ranch houses were assembled. They were expensive despite their appearance and had notable defects (no Levittown efficiency here), but nevertheless the three-bedroom houses were a tremendous success. Brooks personally interviewed every interested buyer and selected the best fit out of the five hundred applications. Because the houses were subsidized, the prices were affordable and values increased rapidly with time.

GUERILLA GARDENING. Hattie Carthan was 64 years old when she started planting trees around Bedford-Stuyvesant in Brooklyn. Over the next twenty years, she got the community involved, planting as well as protecting thousands of trees, and became known as "The Tree Lady of Brooklyn." Everywhere around the city community gardens came into being, mostly on empty lots previously littered with garbage. The very first one was the Liz Christy Community Garden on the corner of Houston Street and Bowery. The garden opened in 1973 and was named after a founder of Green Guerillas, an organization that turns empty lots into gardens.

GRAFFITI. In the early 1980s some 80 percent of subway cars were covered in graffiti. In response, Mayor Koch erected his own Berlin Wall around subway train yards, deploying German shepherds to guard a kill zone between two sets of barbed-wire fences. But more important, and perhaps more effective, were broader changes made by David Gunn, the new MTA president.[35] Any graffiti-bombed train was immediately ordered out of service for cleaning, and trains were regularly repaired and upgraded. This worked pretty well to thwart graffiti taggers, who would receive little satisfaction from seeing their handiwork. By 1988, the system was pretty much graffiti-free.[36]

There were more positive signs of a renaissance in the Bronx a little farther north. **FORDHAM PLAZA [69]** was the first big office building to be built in the borough since the Second World War. The city-owned site sat empty for decades, filled only with litter, despite having great train and subway connections. The development received funds from the whole government trinity—federal, state, and city.

It was designed by Skidmore Owings & Merrill, who were now working in the postmodern style after spending decades building modernist offices worldwide. The thirteen-story cylinder, held by two step-up wings, was clad in yellow brick with dark-glazed brick accents and chrome detailing. The offices were built to such a high specification previously unseen in the Bronx that the rents were double those in the area. It stood empty for two years, but its construction helped to reinvigorate the neighborhood.

There was also growing confidence across the East River in Queens. The borough had lost 100,000 residents in the past decade, but now it was filling up again. Following the 1965 changes in immigration laws, Queens became home to an ever-growing diverse population of immigrants, especially from Asia and Latin America. (Even an African prince came to Queens to find his queen in the 1988 film *Coming to America*.) The new immigrants started countless new businesses and put their children in local schools. The Queens Library became the busiest municipal library system in the whole country.

FORDHAM PLAZA [69]
Skidmore Owings & Merrill
1 Fordham Plaza, Belmont
1986, the Bronx

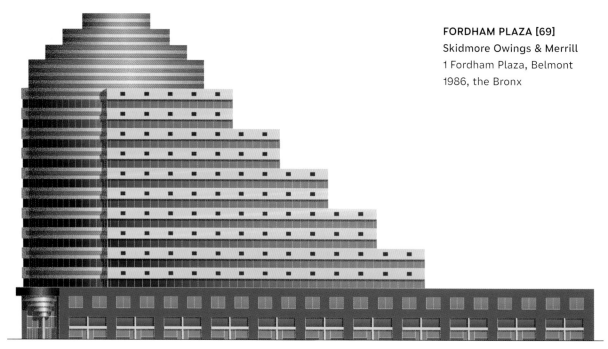

Queens College, which is part of the City University of New York, welcomed many new students, speaking dozens of languages. In the 1980s, the college's Flushing campus was expanded by new buildings, including the **BENJAMIN S. ROSENTHAL LIBRARY [70]** (also known as Queens College Library). Designed by Gruzen Samton Steinglass, the rather conservative six-story building was upstaged by its clock tower. The open structure became the landmark of the campus.

Its official name is rather long—The Chaney-Goodman-Schwerner Clock Tower. It was dedicated to Andrew Goodman, a student at Queens College, and his two friends, who were murdered when trying to register Black voters in the South. Today, there are students from 133 countries speaking 96 different languages. Comedian Jerry Seinfeld and songwriter Carole King are among the school's famous alumni.

**BENJAMIN S. ROSENTHAL
LIBRARY [70]**
(Queens College Library)
Gruzen Samton Steinglass
65-30 Kissena Blvd, Flushing
1988, Queens

Times Square was still a tawdry place that most people avoided, sort of a worm in the Big Apple. The streets were lined with adult movie theaters, peep shows, and legions of sex workers. The surrounding Theater District wasn't doing much better, with many theaters being converted to cinemas or demolished altogether. City hall had attempted to turn things around since the 1960s by banning massage parlors and other like businesses and offering a 20 percent zoning bonus to new construction that incorporated theaters.

MARRIOTT MARQUIS [71] came in like a wrecking ball, wiping out five historic theaters. The hotel's opening was the end of a thirteen-year-long saga that was decided backstage, when a pair of President Reagan's associates pushed the Advisory Council on Historic Preservation to approve the demolitions.[37] The hotel contained a new Marquis theater, but that could hardly balance the loss. The event, however, served as a wake-up call and thrust other threatened Midtown theaters into the spotlight and motivated the decision to list and protect twenty-eight of them.

The hotel was designed as a fortress in what was considered the dangerous frontier of Times Square. The lobby was safely situated on the eighth floor, far from the street. Like a watchtower, a glazed rotating restaurant was built on the roof. The only interaction the hotel had with the street was its huge Kodak screen, an element demanded by zoning on all new Times Square buildings in order to keep its signature neon lights shining. The fifty-story hotel was a blockbuster, and its 1,877 rooms were quickly booked.

Despite its tainted story, the hotel became a catalyst in the renewal of Times Square. Its success inspired construction of four more hotels in the surrounding blocks. New York was cheaper for international visitors than London, Paris, or Tokyo; crowds of tourists began rubbing shoulders with Times Square locals.

The Cold War fizzled away, and where once Bert the Turtle advised children in the 1950s how to survive atomic bomb explosion, the 1990s was the time for *Teenage Mutant Ninja Turtles* (1987–1996), a quartet of evil-fighting reptiles living in sewers of New York City. But the reality was a growing homeless population setting up camp down there. Next to no outside support for patients released en masse from mental hospitals, the shrinking job market, a lack of affordable housing, and a drug epidemic fueled by crack cocaine created a perfect storm leading to an immense homeless crisis. In 1989, New York City spent more money on providing permanent housing for the homeless than the next fifty American cities combined.[38]

MARRIOTT MARQUIS [71]
John Portman, Jr.
1535 Broadway, Times Square
1985, Manhattan

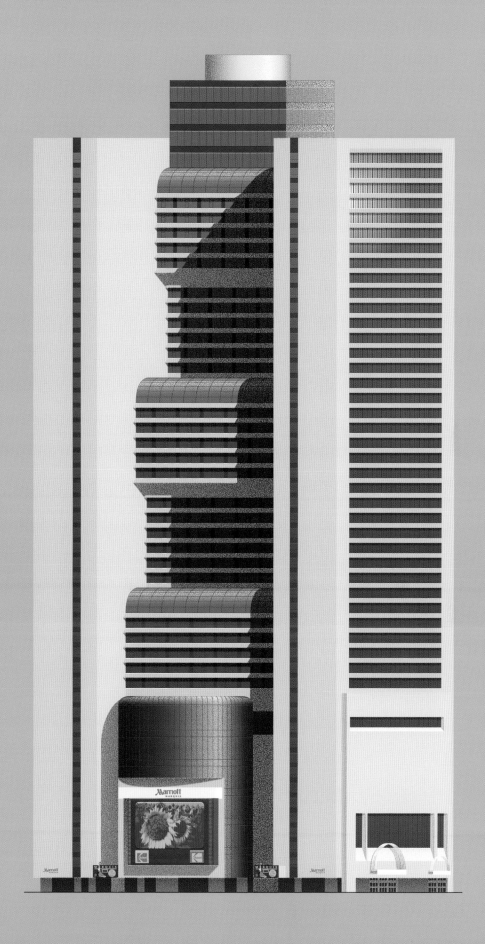

1980s

David Dinkins, the city's first Black mayor, memorably described New York as "a gorgeous mosaic" rather than a melting pot, but he was unable to stop the explosion of racial conflict in the city and served only a single term. He was replaced by Rudy Giuliani, a tough prosecutor who became famous for putting mobsters behind bars, who was ironically a son of a mob enforcer. Giuliani benefited from the thousands of extra police Dinkins hired and crime dropped significantly under his reign.

뉴욕장로교회
NEW YORK PRESBYTARIAN CHURCH

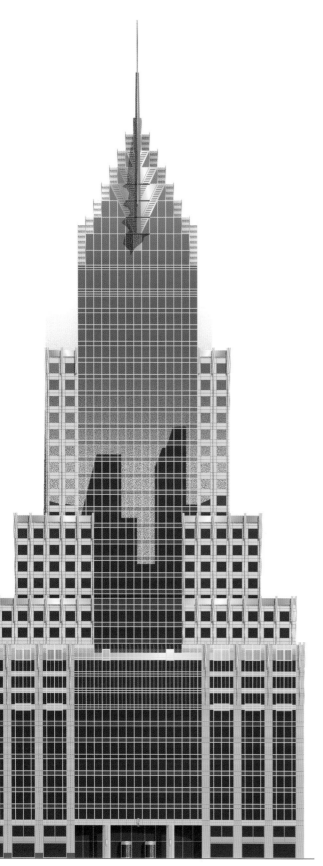

In terms of construction, the early 1990s were slow. The city was still reeling from the 1987 stock market crash, and so nothing went up and office vacancies were high. Some companies even decided to donate their Manhattan buildings to universities in exchange for a tax write-off.

Old buildings had to be upgraded for the new digital age: Electrical systems had to be rewired to feed power-hungry computers, and air conditioning enhanced to take away the extra heat they generated; telecommunication lines had to be added to work with fax machines and the new "information superhighway," a painfully slow Internet in its early days. But in the case of **320 PARK AVENUE [72]** (originally called the Mutual of America Building), the upgrades went much further.

The thirty-year-old building was a run-of-the-mill structure designed by Emery Roth & Sons (who in 1970 had celebrated their one-hundredth postwar Manhattan office building).[39] It was built in the last months of the older, more benevolent zoning code, and thus had some 50 percent more floor space than the current law allowed.[40] So it was absolutely worth refurbishing rather than replacing. The old curtain facade was torn down and the asbestos fireproofing the steel skeleton was stripped away. The structure was slightly reconfigured—its eight wedding-cake-style setbacks were reduced to four, gaining more floor space on the top floors, where the best paying tenants like to roost.

320 PARK AVENUE [72]
Mutual of America Building
Swanke Hayden Connell Architects,
Emery Roth & Sons
320 Park Avenue, Midtown
1995, Manhattan

The low ceilings, a typical shortcoming of midcentury buildings, were partially fixed by reducing the size of overhead air ducts and repositioning the air machinery. The new cladding was originally planned to be stone in postmodern fashion, but because it would have required expensive strengthening of the structure, it was changed to aluminum panels. The most eye-catching new feature was the gabled peak hiding rooftop equipment. Paul Goldberger, architecture critic for the *New York Times*, asked, "Which is worse, honest 1960s cheapness or disingenuous 1990s attempt at art?"

Manhattan became an attractive place for attractive people, or at least that's what TV shows like *Friends* (1994–2004) and *Sex and the City* (1998–2004) seemed to indicate. And just like that all young ambitious people wanted to make it here—again. Places like the Upper East Side were being gentrified, while Greenwich Village and the Upper West Side continued to become trendier and trendier, with rents rising proportionately.

On the Upper West Side, the process had started after the completion of Lincoln Center and was only slowed down, but not stopped, by the economic crises of the 1970s and 1980s. Brownstones were refurbished, while rental apartments and single-room occupancy buildings were turned into condominiums.

THE ALEXANDRIA [73] was, like most new apartment buildings rising on the Upper West Side, built along Broadway. The building occupies a corner site right next to the West Seventy-Second Street subway station. The developer purchased air rights from five surrounding buildings and so was able to add a number of dramatically stepped-up floors. There were 202 apartments in twenty-four stories.

The dynamic facade featured bay windows, a glazed corner tower, and a huge octagonal rooftop box that housed the water tank—all decorated with Egyptian-inspired motifs. The *AIA Guide to New York City* was unusually salty, writing that "Ramses II's mummy may return and terminate this insult to ancient Egypt."

THE ALEXANDRIA [73]
Frank William & Associates, SOM
201 West 72nd St, Upper West Side
1991, Manhattan

One new skyscraper did captivate New Yorkers, but because of its location not its architecture. Indeed, if **ONE COURT SQUARE [74]** (originally the Citigroup Building) stood in Manhattan, no one would have even noticed, but in Queens it was a shocker. Standing between low-rise row houses and garages, the skyscraper looked like it was delivered to the wrong address. It became the tallest building in New York State outside Manhattan for the next twenty-nine years.

Citigroup chose the location for the new building because of its good transport link with their headquarters on Fifty-Third Street, as well as the visual link: The Queens site sat right on an axis with the Manhattan building. The new building was seven times larger than local zoning allowed, but to get the plan approved the bank paid for the renovation of several subway stations, built a pedestrian link between subway lines, and provided space for a branch of Queens Public Library.

Designed by Cuban-born Raúl de Armas of SOM, the building was modest in its styling, if not scale. The fifty stories wrapped in glass and blue-green metal panels were a far cry from the widely recognized 45-degree roof of Citigroup Center. After some time, it became clear that people didn't associate the Queens building with the bank. The solution was the installation of four huge, illuminated logos at the top in what a local man called "a rather ugly font."[41]

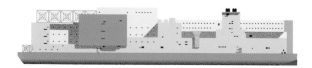

VERNON C. BAIN, PRISON BARGE. The premise of Escape from New York *(1981) was that by the 1990s the whole island of Manhattan would have been converted into a maximum-security prison. The reality proved to be less terrifying, but only slightly. To ease overcrowding at Rikers Island prison, the city purchased two secondhand ships (British troop ships used in the Falklands War) and converted them into floating jails. In 1992, a purpose-built prison barge, the largest in the world, replaced them. Meant to be a temporary solution, the barge remains moored on the shore of Hunts Point in the Bronx to this day.*

ONE COURT SQUARE [74]
(Citigroup Building)
Raúl de Armas of SOM
1 Court Sq, Long Island City
1990, Queens

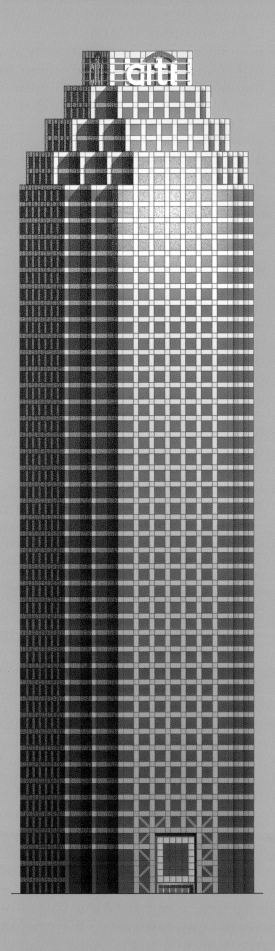

New York City was in the midst of the largest immigration wave in the century, hundreds of thousands of people from China, the Dominican Republic, Korea, Russia, Mexico, Jamaica, India, Pakistan, and Guyana made the city their home. They created new communities and provided talent, capital, and energy to help the Big Apple to blossom again.

Immigrants from Korea were one of the most visible groups, as they opened hundreds of groceries across the city. Several blocks by the Empire State Building became known as Koreatown for the concentration of restaurants dedicated to Korean food. But the majority of Koreans settled in Queens, where they also built most of the city's four hundred Korean churches. The **KOREAN PRESBYTERIAN CHURCH OF QUEENS [75]** (also known as New York Presbyterian Church) was different—it was huge, its architecture was controversial, and it was one of the first buildings designed entirely on a computer.

The church was built in an industrial wasteland at the northern edge of Sunnyside. Commuters whizzing past the site on LIRR trains watched as the tired Art Deco Knickerbocker Laundry from 1932 was being refurbished, extended, and painted black. But the architects placed their main focus on the facade facing the parking lot in the back, because most of the congregation arrived by car. A spacious sanctuary for 2,500 was built on the old laundry's roof, accessed by congregants through a series of wide staircases.

One of the defining features of the megachurch was the distinct canopy structure for one of the staircases. The young architects played with the software used by car designers to create the roof out of a series of shells. The building became one of the most talked about in the whole country, but not everyone was a fan. To architect Alexander Gorlin it looked like "a kind of religious factory attacked by a giant armadillo."

KOREAN PRESBYTERIAN CHURCH OF QUEENS [75]
(New York Presbyterian Church)
Doug Garofalo, Greg Lynn, and Michael McInturf
43-23 37th Avenue, Sunnyside Gardens
1999, Queens

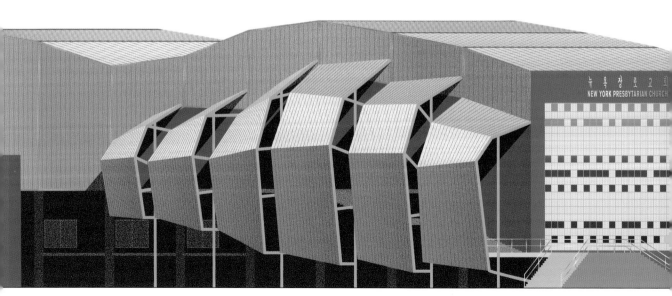

LIGHTHOUSE AND BRIDGE [76] was constructed in 1996 as a part of improvements to Staten Island's St. George waterfront. The open steel structure wasn't properly protected from the rust, which ate away at it, and it had to be demolished in 2018. Designed by Iranian-born artist Siah Armajani, it was built as part of the city's Percent for Art program, which required that 1 percent of the budget for city-funded construction projects be spent on public artwork. The program was one of the periodic attempts to make the area around the ferry terminal more interesting and to hold on to some of the tourists traveling on the ferry, who usually just turn around and go back to Manhattan.

In 1993 Staten Islanders held a referendum and voted overwhelmingly to divorce from New York City. The Fresh Kills Landfill was one of the major reasons. It had been opened in 1947 and was supposed to be only temporary. But as garbage incinerators and landfills in other boroughs shut down, Fresh Kills became the city's only dumping ground. It grew into the world's largest dump and the largest human-made structure by volume. It was inhabited by giant rats and feral dogs. To assuage secessionists, new mayor Rudy Giuliani promised to close the landfill and made the Staten Island Ferry free.[42]

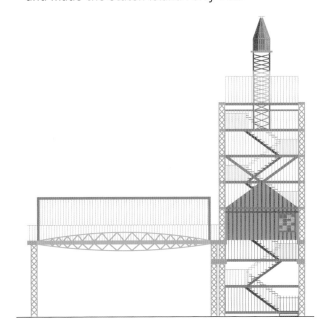

LIGHTHOUSE AND BRIDGE [76]
Siah Armajani
Promenade at Lighthouse
Point, St. George
1996-2018, Staten Island

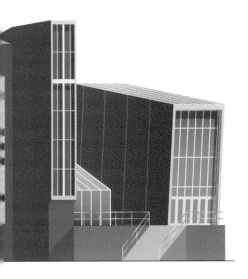

Things were happening in Brooklyn too. The giant Atlantic Center Mall opened at the intersection of Atlantic and Flatbush Avenues and provided some 1,500 jobs (albeit most paid minimum wage). Two subway stations away in downtown Brooklyn rose MetroTech Center, an ambitious project of rebuilding planned as a collaboration between the city, a private developer, and Polytechnic Institute.

Some fifty buildings were demolished to make way for a mixture of educational and commercial buildings. City hall wanted to convert the fading area into the third major business district (after Midtown and downtown) and provide a place where Manhattan-based corporations could outsource their back-office operations instead of going to New Jersey.

The largest of the new buildings, **4 METROTECH [77]**, became the home of J.P. Morgan Chase Bank's computer center. It brought five thousand jobs, most of which were not new but moved from elsewhere in the city. The building was enormous and occupied a full city block. The roofline was defined by huge vents to cool off the machines inside, not unlike 33 Thomas Street. The architects took inspiration in the massing and details of the neighboring Long Island Headquarters of the New York Telephone Company, one of Ralph Walker's Art Deco works. 4 MetroTech now looms over it.

Luring Chase to Brooklyn seemed like a sweet deal at first, but it had a bitter aftertaste when the *New York Times* revealed details of the deal showing that the city gave the bank scandalously high subsidies and even helped them with the electricity bill. The city was desperate to keep the jobs, although there's no knowing if Chase (and other companies taking donations from taxpayers) actually wanted to leave the city in the first place. A major makeover of the whole MetroTech Center was announced in 2022, together with a new name—Brooklyn Commons.

METROCARD. The thin plastic card with a magnetic strip was unveiled in 1993, exactly forty years after the introduction of subway tokens. The city started using tokens for the fare because when it was raised to fifteen cents, the turnstiles couldn't accept two different coins. The MetroCard promised hassle-free travel (given that you swipe it at the right speed and the right angle) without the need to fill your pockets with clunky tokens. A GMC RTS bus was converted into a mobile sales and promotional office and traveled through the city explaining the new system.

4 METROTECH [77]
(Chase Metrotech)
Skidmore Owings & Merrill
4 Metrotech Center, Downtown Brooklyn
1993, Brooklyn

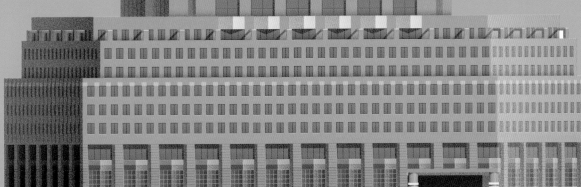

But luckily the city also had some charitable companies and individuals that shared their wealth and supported causes and institutions that struggled because of the city's budget cuts. In the Bronx, the New York Public Library received private funding partially covering a new building for the **SEDGWICK BRANCH NYPL [78]** in Morris Heights. The library could finally start a new chapter by leaving the small space (a converted Chinese restaurant) and moving to a new building that rose on a triangular site on a corner of University Avenue.

Architects David Prendergast and Deborah Laurel, who had previously worked on NYPL branches, decided against completely filling the small site. Instead, they designed an L-shaped layout that left space for a small public plaza filled with a composition of large rocks and posts capped with phosphorescent tops. The tight budget meant that the library was a simple box made out of concrete blocks but attached to it was an eye-catching stainless steel cone that stole the show.

The cone was called a "giant tepee" by Prendergast and contained community space within. It had its own street entrance that allowed it to be used even when the library was closed. The modest library was a success and even made it onto the cover of the prestigious magazine *Architectural Record*. It was clearly overbooked as a couple of years later a second floor dedicated to computers was added.

Public urinators, aggressive panhandlers, fare-beaters, and other characters that were ignored for so long were now actively targeted by the NYPD. In addition, the popularity of crack cocaine declined, demographics changed, and a whole lot of other reasons ultimately led to an impressive reduction in crime. Cafés put tables outside again and people started to go out more, further lowering opportunistic crime.

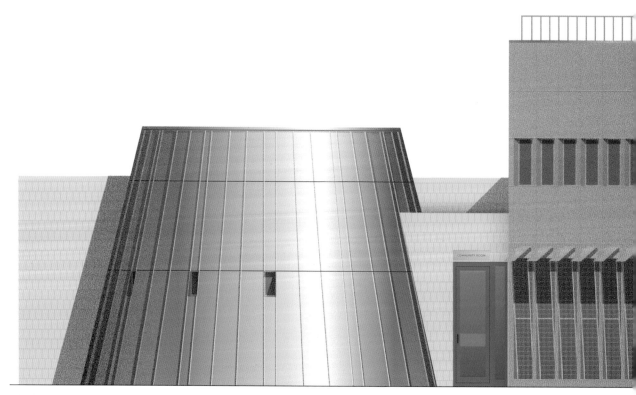

Things were looking up, and a boom in hotel and office construction followed. Something called "new media" (a term encompassing everything from websites to computer games) unexpectedly exploded in New York, a city with a huge pool of talent in advertising, the graphic arts, and publishing.

While hardware and software continued to be developed in California's Silicon Valley, content creation became a huge business in New York and soon employed more people than construction or legal services. But "old media" wasn't doing badly either. Magazine publisher Condé Nast decided to consolidate in a new building on the Crossroads of the World, or Times Square.

Changes at Times Square and Forty-Second Street now seemed to be supercharged, which quickly lost its seediness to become a family-friendly tourist trap: Disney renovated the New Amsterdam Theater to host its musicals, Madame Tussauds wax museum opened on the strip, and McDonald's opened their largest restaurant ever. Probably the most impressive feat of reconfiguration was done by AMC Theatres, which put the ninety-year-old landmarked Empire Theater on rails and moved it 168 feet to use as the lobby for their enormous twenty-five-screen movie theater.

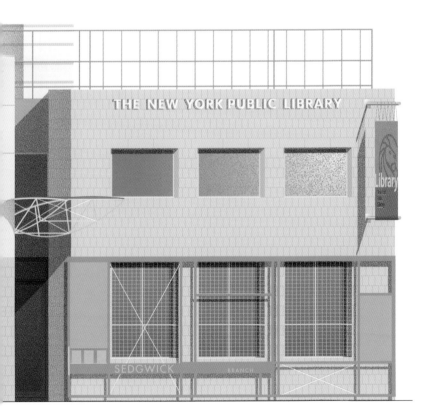

SEDGWICK BRANCH NYPL [78]
(Sedgwick Library)
Prendergast Laurel
1701 Martin Luther King, Jr. Blvd,
Morris Heights
1994, the Bronx

It seemed that the whole area was to be given away to the tourist trade, so it was a shock when Condé Nast announced the move to **4 TIMES SQUARE [79]**. In hindsight, it was a start of a process that made Times Square the corporate capital of popular media.[43] Architects Fox & Fowle designed the complex massed skyscraper in an attempt to fit into the messy context of Times Square. Seen from Bryant Park, the facade was masonry, while from the square itself it was a reflective curtain of glass and a cylinder wrapped in the world's largest LED sign.

It was also one of America's first skyscrapers using green technology to make it more sustainable. Solar panel cells were integrated in the facade and gas-powered fuel cells provided 8 percent of needed electricity. Mechanical ventilation (instead of air conditioning) further reduced energy consumption.[44]

Things were interesting at the top as well: A hat truss, which stiffens the building by tying external columns to the core, was left exposed, and the top was attached to a communication tower. The tower was a textbook case of Russian Constructivism appropriated by the capitalist machine. Frank Gehry, the world's most famous architect at the time, also designed a nice cafeteria for staffers, who wouldn't have to fight the tourist crowds at lunchtime.

CHEVROLET CAPRICE. Changes in the way cabs were leased made taxi drivers into so-called independent contractors. Drivers were squeezed by paying not only for the daily use of the cab, but for gasoline, repairs, and lease fees. They were working more hours for less money, making the job more attractive to people with fewer job opportunities—new immigrants. Russian, Indian, and Pakistani drivers took over.[45]

4 TIMES SQUARE [79]
(Condé Nast Building)
Fox & Fowle
4 Times Square, Times Square
1999, Manhattan

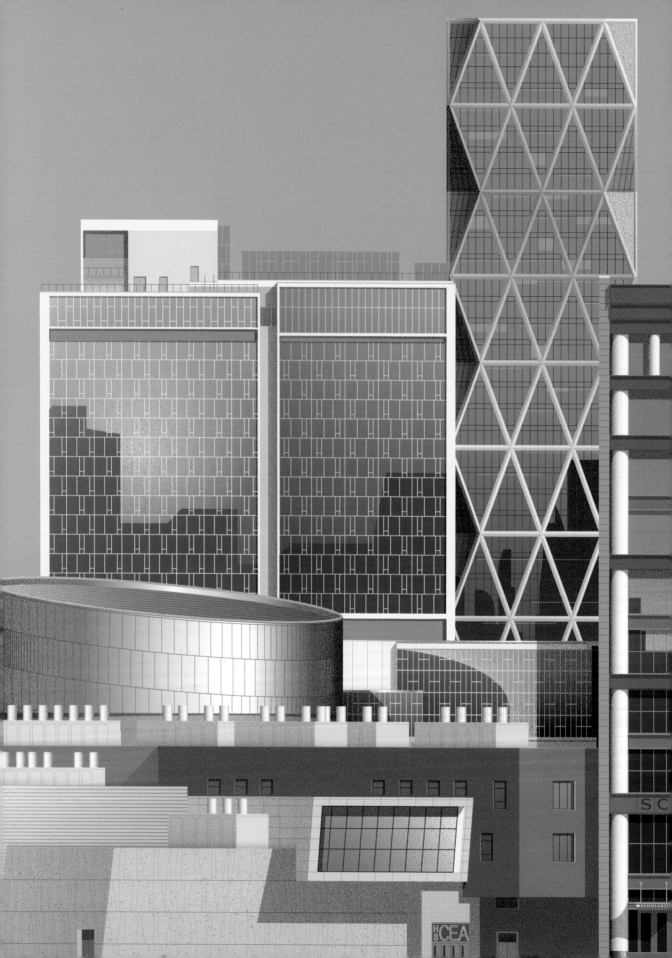

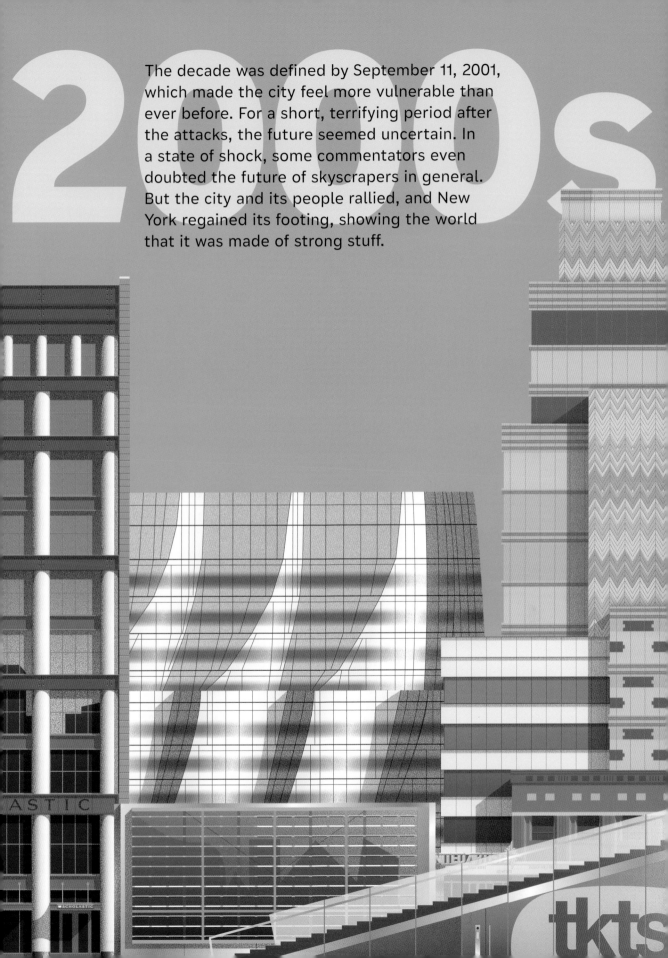

2000s

The decade was defined by September 11, 2001, which made the city feel more vulnerable than ever before. For a short, terrifying period after the attacks, the future seemed uncertain. In a state of shock, some commentators even doubted the future of skyscrapers in general. But the city and its people rallied, and New York regained its footing, showing the world that it was made of strong stuff.

On the morning of September 11, 2001, a group of Islamic terrorists hijacked four airplanes, crashing a pair of them into the Twin Towers of the World Trade Center. The buildings survived the initial collision, despite the destruction of large parts of their load-bearing facades. However, the thin fireproofing of their steel skeleton had been blown off by the impact and left no protection against the flames fed by the huge amount of aviation fuel that soaked the structures.

In a race against time, firefighters, police, and members of the public rushed to help evacuate the buildings. After almost an hour of intense fire, the South Tower suddenly collapsed, its steel structure fatally weakened by the blaze. The North Tower stood for forty minutes longer before also collapsing. Once 110 stories tall, the lightweight skyscrapers compressed into a pile of rubble a mere ten stories tall. The whole world watched this on live TV in absolute horror.

A third hijacked airplane hit the Pentagon, and the last one crashed in Pennsylvania, short of its intended target—Washington, DC. In total, 2,977 people lost their lives, the majority of them in New York City. But there were no crazed stampeding mobs as seen in catastrophic movies. Most people stayed collected and helped one another. Teachers in Lower Manhattan took schoolchildren to their homes. Strangers hugged in the streets. Restaurants gave out food and drink to first responders.

Mayor Giuliani, whose approval ratings before the event were dismal (he was sometimes referred to as the Mussolini of Manhattan), showed leadership and became known as the Mayor of America. The Twin Towers, despite being seen as symbols of New York, were appreciated as never before. Now they were on par with religious icons. A church in Brooklyn's Dyker Heights built a statue of a kneeling Jesus cradling the two towers.

Among the victims were 343 FDNY firefighters, 37 officers of the Port Authority Police Department, and 23 from the NYPD. But it wasn't over yet. Ground Zero was on fire. The air was full of smoke and dust containing particles of PCBs, lead, and asbestos. Thousands of rescue, recovery, and clean-up workers would end up with lifelong health problems.

The city was in trouble. Despite the outpouring of support—or as satirical newspaper *The Onion* wrote, "Rest of Country Temporarily Feels Deep Affection for New York"—the future didn't look rosy. In the three months after the attack, New York City lost some 430,000 jobs and another 18,000 small businesses were destroyed or displaced. Tourism, one of the city's most important industries, shrank by half.

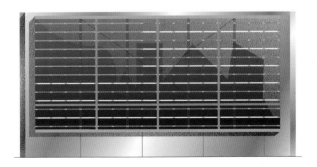

US ARMED SERVICES RECRUITMENT STATION. This small kiosk in Times Square, designed by the Architecture Research Office, is basically a box made of glass and stainless steel. Fluorescent light tubes in the window form the US flag, and the open-plan interior is split into four cubicles, one for each of the armed services—Army, Air Force, Marines, and Navy. Following the attacks of 9/11, the kiosk was besieged by people wanting to enlist.

It was a tough start for the new mayor, Michael Bloomberg. Born in Boston, Bloomberg made billions by developing software that provided financial news to Wall Street traders. He financed his political campaigns out of his own pocket and so had more flexibility to set his agenda than most politicians. His vision of New York as a "luxury city" led to the biggest change in its fabric since the time of mass urban renewal, and not all of it was for the better.

The Meatpacking District, a postindustrial sanctuary for galleries and clubs rent-hiked out of SoHo, underwent a complete transformation. The unlikely spark of the redevelopment boom was a decaying elevated railway dating back to the 1930s that spanned the area. Unused for two decades, nature had reclaimed it.

Naturally seeded by wind and birds, wild grasses, flowers, and bushes flourished between its rusting tracks. But property prices were growing too. People owning land under this High Line wanted to see it gone so they could build higher. Demolition was approved but halted at the last minute thanks to a campaign by two locals who managed to get the support of city hall.

But the city didn't have any spare money to buy out the property owners and came up with a creative solution. They created special zoning that allowed the transfer of the air rights across the whole of the west Chelsea neighborhood (usually it's only possible to transfer to adjoining sites). This meant that the property owners below the High Line could sell their unused air rights to the highest bidder and make easy money without building anything.

Once the process of turning the High Line into an urban park started, developers saw the green (as in dollars) possibilities. **THE STANDARD [80]** was one of the first to take advantage. The hotel's chunky concrete legs straddled the path and held fourteen stories of hotel rooms that often exposed guests in their rooms. The architects stated that the semi-opaque glazing standard for hotels was swapped for extra-transparent glass that catered "to the certain desire for exhibitionism."

TKTS TIMES SQUARE. The redesign for this small booth selling discount tickets for Broadway and off-Broadway shows was selected in the largest architecture competition in New York's history, attracting 683 entrants from 31 countries.[46] The winner, architecture firm Choi Ropiha, designed a red-tiered staircase that served as both a roof and a platform with views of Times Square. What a better place for people-watching than at The Crossroads of the World?

THE STANDARD [80]
(The Standard, High Line)
Ennead Architects
848 Washington St, Chelsea
2009, Manhattan

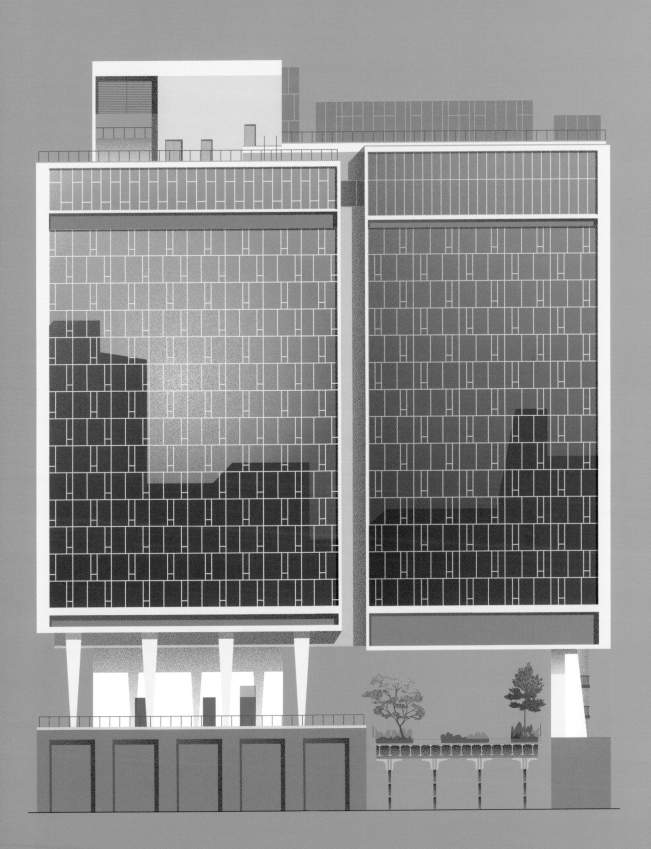

But thankfully not all new buildings were kitted out this way. **IAC BUILDING [81]**, albeit fully glazed, used fritted glass—which makes it look like it was sprayed with white paint. Not only does this offer privacy for the tenants, but it limits solar gain and thus saves energy. It was Gehry's first building in New York, and it stands out in his portfolio, as it didn't use his typical stainless steel cladding.

IAC's boss, Barry Diller, was intensely involved in the design and demanded the use of the white glass. The result was arguably one of Gehry's best buildings. Built on a block that the High Line cuts through, it was finished a couple of years before the first stage of the park opened and the redevelopment bonanza began. With the neighborhood still seen as a backwater, at least Diller was close to his yacht, which was moored on the Hudson River. But in just a couple of years, buildings by the likes of Jean Nouvel, Renzo Piano, and Zaha Hadid were springing up around the High Line.

IAC BUILDING [81]
Frank Gehry
555 West 18th St, Chelsea
2007, Manhattan

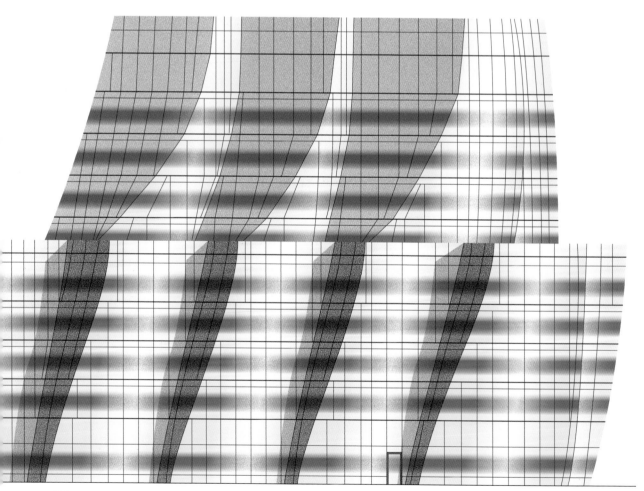

In SoHo, the neighborhood was already finishing its conversion from arty to luxe, but there was still some potential for something new. The **SCHOLASTIC BUILDING [82]** was proof of that. A publisher of educational books, Scholastic wanted to expand and purchased a site neighboring their offices. Normally this wouldn't be a problem in most places in the city, however this was the SoHo-Cast Iron Historic District, a protected area concentrating buildings with unique cast-iron facades.

The history of the site itself was a good illustration of the need for protecting such buildings. A beautiful five-story iron-cast building had once stood here, but it was demolished in 1954 (two decades before establishment of the district) and replaced by a lowly garage. Now there was a chance to add the missing teeth.

Anything new built here had to be approved by the Landmarks Preservation Commission. To impress them, respected Italian architect Aldo Rossi was brought on board. It was a good bet: His design charmed the commission and was approved after only an hour of deliberation. Rossi refused to imitate old facades and their intricate details and instead chose to reinterpret them in an inventive and subtle way. Unfortunately, however, Rossi was fatally injured in a car accident shortly after, and the final plans had to be finished by his partner, Morris Adjmi.

SCHOLASTIC BUILDING [82]
Aldo Rossi, Morris Adjmi
557 Broadway, SoHo
2001, Manhattan

Another European architect brought in to grace the streets of Manhattan was Englishman Norman Foster, the designer of **HEARST TOWER [83]**, although he didn't bring with him any Old-World sensibility. The tower was a redevelopment of William Randolph Hearst's landmarked 1928 International Magazine Building designed by Austrian architect and set designer Joseph Urban. The six-story building was always expected to be extended by additional floors, but every attempt had failed until now. Foster designed a striking forty-six-story skyscraper shooting up from the old building. The landmarked facade was left intact, but the interior floors were completely gutted, creating a three-story glass-roofed atrium. The entrance features *Icefall*, a waterfall sculpture fed by collected rainwater.

The skyscraper was lauded as the first in New York to receive LEED Gold and later, after recertification, Platinum rating. It was built using recycled steel and collected rainwater for use in cooling systems. And all of the materials used for the open-plan cubicles were sustainably sourced.

The triangulated honeycomb structure was not only beautiful to look at, but also required 20 percent less steel than traditional construction. However, cleaning the tower glass and its recessed corners wasn't an easy task—it took some three years to develop "New York's most complex window washing crane" in order to do it. However in 2013, the scaffolding broke on the crane, stranding a pair of unlucky window cleaners. A hole had to be cut into one of the windows on the forty-fourth floor to bring them inside.

FORD CROWN VICTORIA. The Ford Crown Victoria was New York's universal taxi after the Chevrolet Caprice was discontinued in the 1990s. Changing population demographics and dismal conditions for cabbies meant that by 2004 over 90 percent of medallion drivers were foreign-born.[47]

WALK/DON'T WALK. Pedestrian traffic lights were redesigned to symbols after half a century. The lettering was replaced with a walking person in white that alternated with a raised hand in red.

HEARST TOWER [83]
Foster + Partners, Joseph Urban
300 West 57th St, Midtown
2006, Manhattan

In Brooklyn, Bruce Ratner, developer behind the 1990s Brooklyn MetroTech, purchased a run-down adult movie theater in Brooklyn Heights and replaced it with **110 COURT STREET [84]**. Ratner was always being criticized for the lack of architectural quality in his projects, and so he commissioned award-winning office Hardy Holzman Pfeiffer Associates to design the thirteen-story cinema complex.

The architects clad the vertical stack of windowless screening halls in tiles arranged in a wild mix of patterns, giving it an enigmatic appearance. But nothing could soften the overbearing size of the building. The movie theater was known for rowdy screenings, where shouting, food fights, and even fistfights between the patrons weren't uncommon.

A large Barnes & Noble bookshop and a Starbucks on the ground floor signaled the area was gentrifying. The once-high crime rate that kept businesses away from the area faded away—between 1994 and 2002 murders there had declined by 72 percent.[48] It was a similar situation across much of the city.

JFK AIRTRAIN. New York is the only global city that doesn't have a one-seat ride from the airport to the city center. The AirTrain hoped to remedy that, but it still didn't link up any major area airport directly with Manhattan. The eight-mile-long elevated railway was eventually built and connected airport terminals and parking lots at JFK with subway stations in Howard Beach and Jamaica in Queens.[49]

110 COURT STREET [84]
Hardy Holzman
Pfeiffer Associates
100 Court Street,
Brooklyn Heights
2000, Brooklyn

UNITEDARTISTS

NAUZOOGAY   CAST AWAY

SNATCH   MEMENTO

REQUIEM FOR A DREAM   ROAD TRIP   AMERICAN PSYCHO

TRAFFIC   THE BEACH   DUDE, WHERE'S MY CAR?

BARNES & NOBLE

BOOKSELLERS

**BRONXWORKS CLASSIC
COMMUNITY CENTER [85]**
(Melrose Community Center)
Agrest & Gandelsonas
286 E 156th St, Melrose
2001, the Bronx

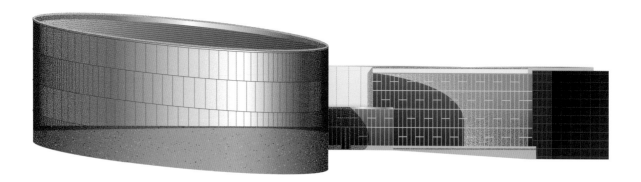

Melrose in the South Bronx had been devastated during the 1970s and 1980s by arson and neglect. In the early 1990s, the city published plans to rebuild the area, but locals, living in the remaining buildings, were having none of it. Yolanda García and other activists fought against the displacement the renewal plan would bring and founded Nos Quedamos/We Stay, a group that would lead a more sustainable and fairer revitalization of the neighborhood.

BRONXWORKS CLASSIC COMMUNITY CENTER [85] (originally Melrose Community Center) was built on a parking lot of NYCHA's Melrose Houses. It also served nearby Jackson Houses and Morrisania Air Rights (one of the less creatively named housing projects). It was designed by Diana Agres, an Argentinian-born architect and writer. The oval gymnasium was tough in appearance, clad in metal and set on a concrete base. In contrast, the two-story block with classrooms was richly glazed to bring in lots of natural light and to allow bored students to watch life on Morrison Avenue outside.

As the population in the city grew, the number of available apartments (never high to start with) dwindled. Owners of detached houses in the outer boroughs, especially Queens, started to convert their basements to apartments, many of which were illegal. These apartments gave new immigrants, low-income families, and the elderly a place to live, but they routinely lacked basic fire protection and could become death traps during flash floods. The basement units and their residents are usually not registered with the city, making census data inaccurate. This in turn leads to the wrong amount being allocated to services like garbage collection and to overcrowding in certain school districts.

The **HIGH SCHOOL FOR CONSTRUCTION TRADES, ENGINEERING AND ARCHITECTURE [86]** opened at the intersection of Ozone Park, Richmond Hill, and Woodhaven in Queens to help with overcrowding. The new building, by Miami-based architecture studio Arquitectonica, was designed using an unusual amount of materials and construction technologies—for the sake of providing students with practical examples. The school is separated into blocks defined by external materials—bricks for classrooms and offices, exposed concrete for the auditorium, metal cladding for drafting labs, and yellow paneling for the library.

With great power comes great responsibility, but not everyone takes this seriously. Deregulated Wall Street was making astronomic profits with multiple high-risk schemes. In 2008, it all came crashing down. This Wall Street crash, not relegated only to New York City, created a global economic crisis. Most top-positioned bankers didn't even understand the highly complex and extremely risky ploys they were making money on, but the taxpayer came to the rescue and bailed them out and then it would eventually be business as usual again.

HIGH SCHOOL FOR CONSTRUCTION TRADES, ENGINEERING AND ARCHITECTURE [86]
Arquitectonica
94-06 104th St, Ozone Park
2006, Queens

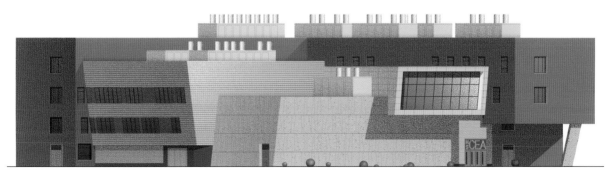

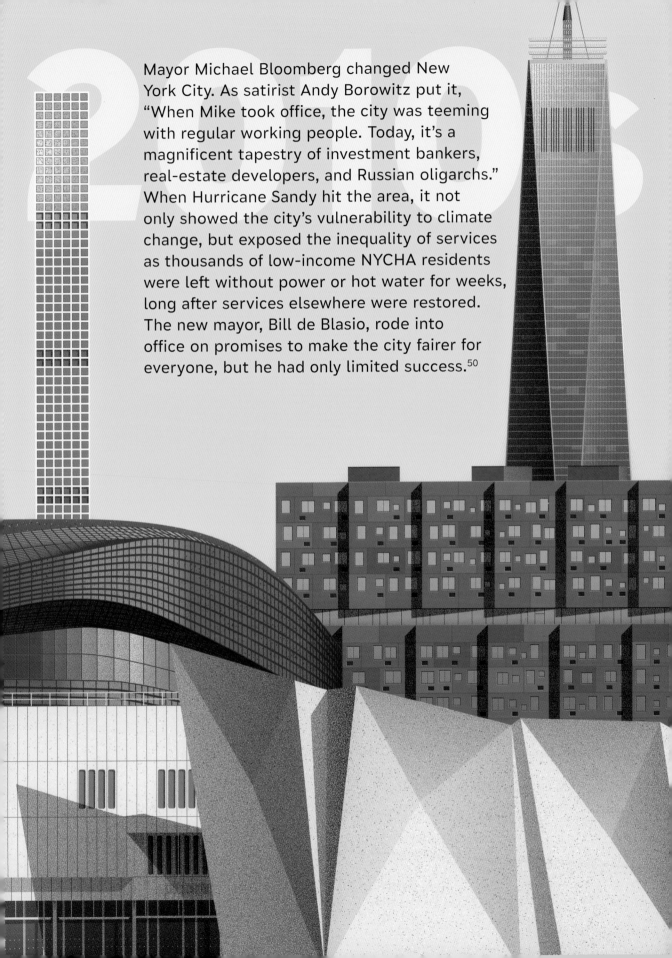

Mayor Michael Bloomberg changed New York City. As satirist Andy Borowitz put it, "When Mike took office, the city was teeming with regular working people. Today, it's a magnificent tapestry of investment bankers, real-estate developers, and Russian oligarchs." When Hurricane Sandy hit the area, it not only showed the city's vulnerability to climate change, but exposed the inequality of services as thousands of low-income NYCHA residents were left without power or hot water for weeks, long after services elsewhere were restored. The new mayor, Bill de Blasio, rode into office on promises to make the city fairer for everyone, but he had only limited success.[50]

The pile at Ground Zero was still smoking when issues regarding the rebuilding surfaced. A battle raged between landowner the Port Authority, leaseholder Larry Silverman, and the planning authority representing the city. In addition, the state and the families of the victims all had their ideas of what to do with the site.

The leaseholder wanted to make as much profit off the office space as possible, while the planners saw a chance to transform the damaged area into a more mixed-use neighborhood since so many jobs had migrated uptown even before 9/11 and the area was virtually empty in the evenings and on weekends. A huge international competition for the masterplan of the area was held. Uruguayan architect Rafael Viñoly came out as the clear favorite.

But Governor George Pataki intervened and picked a scheme by Daniel Libeskind. The Polish-born architect still had vivid memories of arriving at New York harbor from Europe when he was thirteen. He was the only architect who had actually visited Ground Zero. Libeskind was certain Viñoly had won the competition and was on his way to the airport when he heard he had been chosen instead.[51]

But the drama wasn't over. The leaseholder wasn't at all happy with the plan and brought one of the most esteemed corporate architects in the country, Princeton-born David Childs of SOM, to redesign it. The forced compromise resulted in **ONE WORLD TRADE CENTER [87]** (or the Freedom Tower). The design was revised again with feedback from NYPD antiterrorist experts: All the lower floors had to be fortified in thick concrete and steel.

CITI BIKE. After a 1979 visit to China, where then-mayor Koch saw how the people went everywhere on bikes, he suggested New Yorkers should try to do the same. It was considered an absurd idea. Fast-forward more than thirty years. Citi Bike, a bicycle sharing program, is introduced in 2013 and becomes a runaway success. Bike stations were located mostly in Manhattan and parts of Brooklyn and Queens. The network was eventually expanded to the Bronx. However, Staten Island still remains out of the loop.

ONE WORLD TRADE CENTER [87]
(Freedom Tower)
David Childs, Daniel Libeskind
285 Fulton St, Financial District
2014, Manhattan

The skyscraper's height of 1,776 feet referenced the year the Declaration of Independence was signed. There was a lot of controversy regarding the official height, since the 408-foot spire was counted in as an integral part of the building. The Quebec-made spike was originally intended to be covered in fiberglass sheeting to make it look more like a part of the building.

However, the sheeting was dropped to save money, and now it looks like a giant toothpick has been stuck into the flat roof. The building became the tallest in the United States and the Western Hemisphere. Buildings in Asia and the Middle East were already too high into the sky for it to be competitive on the global stage.

The new **WORLD TRADE CENTER STATION (PATH) [88]** (also known as the Oculus) was probably the only section of inspired architecture on the site. Santiago Calatrava, a Spanish architect and structural engineer, designed what could be described as a retail cathedral that doubles as a terminal station for New Jersey trains. To enjoy it, one must push away the thoughts of how many dilapidated subway stations could be fixed up for the eye-watering $4 billion it cost to build.

WTC STATION (PATH) (88)
(Oculus)
Santiago Calatrava
70 Vesey Street, Financial District
2016, Manhattan

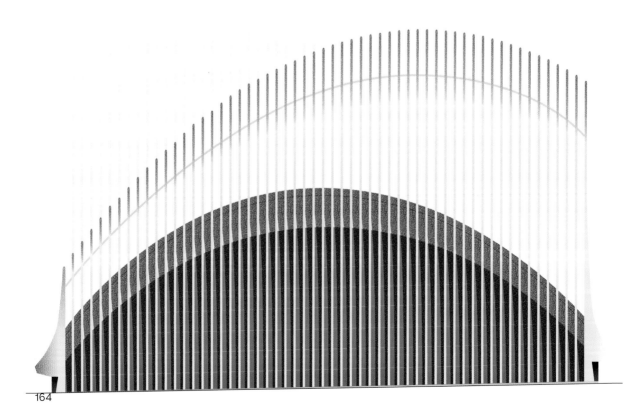

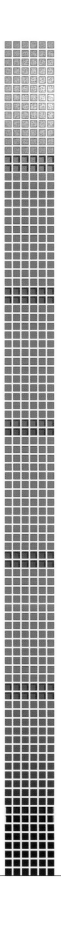

Oligarchs, ultra-rich individuals thanks to close links to governments, siphon wealth from their countries to invest abroad. This flow of dirty money is joined by tributaries from corrupt politicians and criminals, ultimately leading to the estuaries of London, Singapore, and New York where they translate into luxury real estate purchases. Along the way, a niche group of lawyers, accountants, and realtors wet their beaks.

That's about the only benefit the cities get from the process. Most of these investment apartments were not lived in more than a couple of times per year, if ever. Purchased in cash through shell companies, the buyers would remain anonymous and pay little, if any, tax. **432 PARK TOWER [89]** by Rafael Viñoly was built to fulfil the demand for such residences. Briefly the tallest residential building in the world, the tower was constructed using technologies that didn't exist when the city's building codes were written.

Meanwhile, more super-tall structures with apartments owned by Russians, Chinese, and Saudis, began popping up on the northern edge of Central Park, nicknamed Billionaires' Row, and casting a mile-long shadow over the park. There are reports of owners complaining about the defects of such structures caused by swaying in the wind—such as groaning of the walls, broken water pipes, and malfunctioning elevators.

432 PARK TOWER [89]
Rafael Viñoly, SLCE Architects
432 Park Avenue, Midtown
2015, Manhattan

Some slightly more affordable housing was constructed in the outer boroughs, made possible by rezoning. Incredibly, 40 percent of the city was rezoned during Bloomberg's time as mayor. He successfully used rezoning as a tool to increase the city's revenue after 9/11. Areas around existing subway stations, neighborhood centers, and the waterfront were upzoned to allow for taller and larger buildings. This gave rise to multiple mini-Manhattans in the outer boroughs.

In Queens, after years of standing tall and lonely, Citigroup Center was finally surrounded by equal construction. In Long Island City, the once-industrial Hunter's Point waterfront was rezoned to allow a dense pack of tall residential buildings. **HUNTER'S POINT LIBRARY [90]**, albeit dwarfed by these new blocks, attracts the most attention. It's a flagship branch of Queens Public Library.

Steven Holl, a Washington-born architect based in New York, designed the building with a surprisingly small footprint and organized everything vertically in six stories. Seemingly randomly shaped windows frame stunning views of Manhattan on every floor, and the open interior space flows playfully upward. But this novel concept created the issue of accessibility—there were too many stairs and only a single elevator. Despite this, it's a hugely successful building, showing a possible model for future libraries that perhaps allows for less space for physical books and more space to sit and study.

NISSAN NV200 TAXI. In 2011, the van was chosen as the "Taxi of Tomorrow," and taxi owners were required to purchase one. The compact van offered more legroom and seating than the Crown Victoria sedan and included luxuries like passenger airbags and USB charging and was wheelchair accessible. But the maintenance cost on the vans was expensive, and taxi owners resented being forced to buy them. After seven years, the rules were changed, and the city expanded the list of approved vehicle models to thirty.

HUNTER'S POINT LIBRARY [90]
Steven Holl Architects
47-40 Center Blvd, Hunter's Point
2019, Queens

In Williamsburg, Brooklyn's hippest neighborhood, rose **ONE SOUTH FIRST AND TEN GRAND [91]**. As its name suggests, it houses two interlocking elements—offices and apartments—that are separated by a dramatic gap that is perhaps a symbol of the need for work-life balance. At forty-six floors, it was by far the tallest building in Williamsburg. The building has a number of modern amenities, including a rooftop pool and a pet-grooming station.

Of the 330 units, 25 percent were made affordable to comply with zoning. The building sits on what was the famous Domino Sugar Refinery, which operated there for 150 years. Standing just north of Williamsburg Bridge, the large site is being redeveloped with multiple residential towers and a green space called Domino Park. The main refinery building, a dark brick giant punctuated with a central smokestack dating back to 1883, is listed as a landmark and is planned to be repurposed.

With the seemingly never-ending influx of New Yorkers to the borough, it was reported in 2014 that Brooklyn became the least affordable place to buy a home in the whole country. The borough has been a victim of its own success. With its microbreweries, postindustrial chic, and love of anything artisanal, Brooklyn became world famous and its vibe has been replicated around the globe. In just the first half of the 2010s, 132,000 people made the borough their home.

**ONE SOUTH FIRST
AND TEN GRAND [91]**
COOKFOX
1 S 1st St, Williamsburg
2019, Brooklyn

STATEN ISLAND FERRY, JOHN F. KENNEDY. Built in the amply named Texas town of Orange, the orange-colored ferry was commissioned in 1965 and served Staten Islanders for half a century. When it was decommissioned in 2022, the ferry was purchased at auction by Staten Island natives and Saturday Night Live *alums Pete Davidson and Colin Jost for $125,000.[52] They are planning to turn it into a floating comedy club and entertainment venue.*

Even the friendly neighborhood superhero, who had always been associated with Queens, got a Brooklyn address in 2018's *Spider-Man: Into the Spider-Verse*. Brooklyn also finally became home to a major league team a half century after the Dodgers moved to California in 1957. (Many old-timers are still angry about that, especially coming just two years after the team beat the rival Yankees in the World Series.) Between Robert Moses blocking a proposed new site for the ballpark and low attendance figures because people were flocking to the suburbs, there was just no place for the beloved team in Brooklyn anymore.

BARCLAYS ARENA [92] was built at almost the exact same spot as the 1955 proposed ballpark site—at the intersection of Atlantic and Flatbush Avenues, over the LIRR Vanderbilt Railyard. Its developer had also purchased the Nets, a basketball team based in New Jersey, and moved them to Brooklyn. With the involvement of billionaire megastar rapper (and Beyoncé's husband) Jay-Z, the project was a slam dunk. Jay-Z became the arena's biggest booster and even helped with the design of the team's new jerseys.

Jay-Z also owned a tiny portion of the arena and the Brooklyn Nets. His involvement gave the project credibility in the community, and he turned his star power on it with a week-long string of concerts. The arena was also part of a wider development that was substantially changed after the 2008 economic crash—more luxury pads and less office jobs for locals. Meanwhile, the majority ownership was bounced to a Russian oligarch, who later passed it on to a Chinese billionaire.

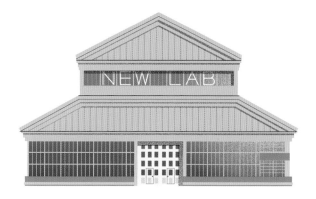

NEWLAB AT THE BROOKLYN YARD. Manufacturing made a return to the Brooklyn Navy Yard. But now instead of building ships, the site will be dealing in high-tech robotics and artificial intelligence. Marvel Architects refashioned a century-old navy industrial complex into a hub for some six hundred tech whiz kids. Steiner Studios took over part of the yard and built the country's largest film and TV studios outside of Hollywood.

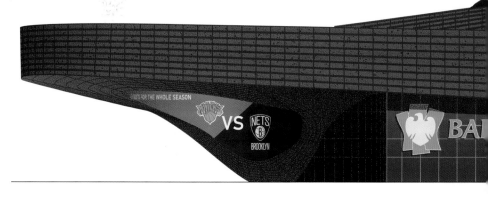

BARCLAYS ARENA [92]
SHoP
620 Atlantic Ave, Prospect Heights
2012, Brooklyn

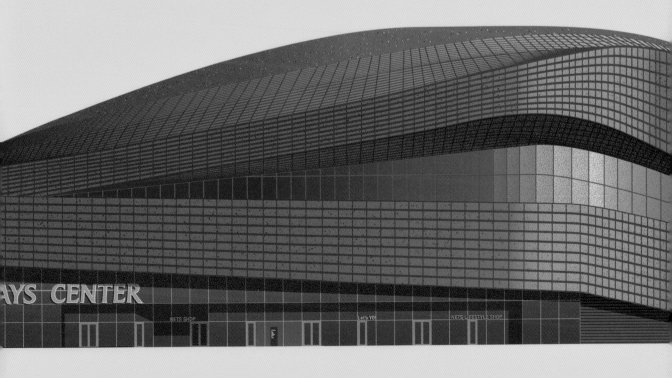

VIA VERDE [93]
Grimshaw + Dattner
Architects
700 Brook Ave, Woodstock
2012, the Bronx

The Bronx is the least healthy county in the whole of New York State, and **VIA VERDE [93]** (or Green Way) was a revolutionary new housing development in the South Bronx's Woodstock neighborhood that was an attempt to help that through architecture. It is a product of a competition, run in association with the New York Chapter of AIA, that was looking for a new model of sustainable and healthy housing.

The Via Verde staircases were designed to receive a lot of natural light and were placed next to entrances to encourage tenants to walk up instead of using elevators. The gym was situated in a prime spot on the roof terrace that affords great views and plenty of light. As befitting its name, an orchard and container gardens offer opportunities to not only interact with nature but to socialize with other tenants, which can help improve mental health.

The social mix is a key part of the project. Of the 222 residential units, 30 percent were sold to middle-income households. The rest were low- and moderate-income rentals. Apart from one-floor apartments, there are also duplexes and even town houses. The units have two exposures, and the cross-ventilation reduces the need for air conditioning. There are solar panels on the roof, and rainwater is also collected and reused. Despite the success of the project, it would be difficult to replicate it on a grand scale, but there are great ideas that can be copied by other developments.

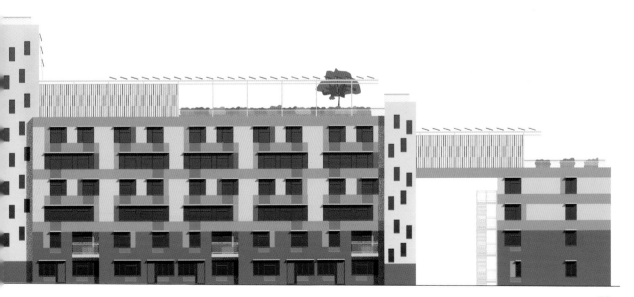

SUGAR HILL DEVELOPMENT [94]
David Adjaye
898 St Nicholas Ave, Harlem
2014, Manhattan

Another visionary project was **SUGAR HILL DEVELOPMENT [94]** in upper Manhattan. Named after the neighborhood on the border of Harlem and Washington Heights, the charcoal (or gunmetal) building raised many eyebrows. While it was under construction, some locals thought it was another luxury development but, on the contrary, it was actually built as affordable housing for low-income families, the homeless, and recovering addicts. The development also included an early childhood center and houses the Children's Museum of Art & Storytelling.

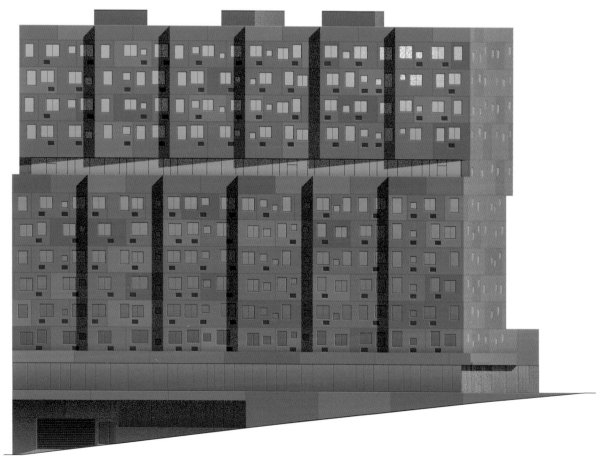

Sugar Hill was the brainchild of the Broadway Housing Communities (BHC), a nonprofit organization run by Ellen Baxter. Baxter had created housing for thousands of low-income families and special-needs people for the past thirty years. There were 48,000 applications for the 124 apartments—a testimony to the dire need for affordable housing in the city. The construction was paid for by a cross-agency effort as well as with philanthropic funds.

BHC hired Tanzanian-born British architect David Adjaye, who designed an unapologetically bold building. He didn't want it to fit in, but instead to become a proud new landmark of the neighborhood. When his design was criticized for not being attractive enough, Adjaye asked, "Why is it that this is 'cool' for rich people but 'tough' for poor people?"

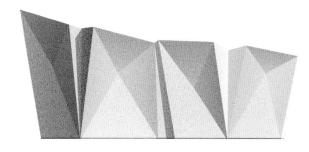

DSNY SPRING STREET SALT SHED. Designed by Dattner Architects and WXY, the cubist ice-blue shed stores salt used for snow removal by the DSNY. On the north end of TriBeCa, the impressive $24 million shed is 69 feet tall and can store up to 5,000 tons of salt. Its massive six-foot-thick walls can withstand almost any kind of cataclysmic attack. The architects even imagined visitors in the distant future stumbling upon the shed the same way the hero of 1968's Planet of the Apes *encounters the Statue of Liberty.*

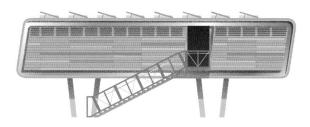

NYC PARKS BEACH RESTORATION MODULES. Hurricane Sandy destroyed thousands of homes and other structures on the city's coastline and cruelly exposed the need to rethink the city's use of flood zones. Garrison Architects designed modular units that can be easily modified to use as comfort stations, lifeguard towers, and offices. Factory-built, the solar-powered modules were installed in 37 locations around the city, including Rockaway Beach, Coney Island, and Cedar Grove Beach on Staten Island, and are also flood-proof.

With crime rates dropping since the 1990s, applications to New York City universities skyrocketed. Columbia University, one of the most prestigious private schools of higher education in the world, saw an increase in student applications. Its campus in Morningside Heights was gradually expanded after the Second World War, but as the neighborhood around it slowly deteriorated, relations between the university and its neighbors became strained.

Tensions ultimately came to a head in 1968 when Columbia proposed building a student gym in the city-owned Morningside Park, but only opening 12 percent of it to the public. There was also an element of segregation to the proposal, as locals would have to enter through a bottom door rather than the front door for students. Students organized a mass protest, with flyers declaring, "The big steal is on." Protestors occupied campus buildings, which resulted in a lockdown.

The university eventually backed down and the gym wasn't built. The protest resulted in students, especially Black students, getting a greater voice in future university decisions. Columbia learned its lesson and started to be more involved with the surrounding community, including when developing its new Manhattanville campus. It hired Italian architect Renzo Piano to design the masterplan with an open European-style campus that was in contrast to the typical American walled-off typology. **THE FORUM AT COLUMBIA UNIVERSITY [95]** was one of the first buildings to be completed. Its ground floor is an open and accessible workspace, like a nice cafe where you don't have to buy anything to work on your laptop. The upper floors contain meeting rooms and conference theaters.

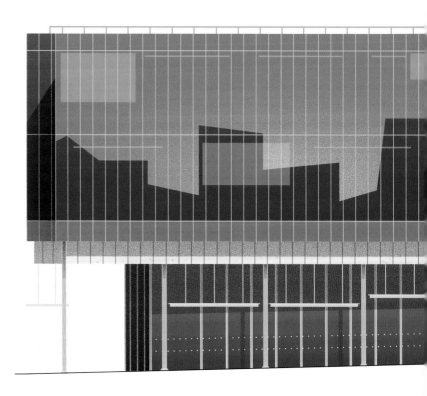

Once finished, the campus will be the first in the country to receive a LEED Platinum certification, a rating that measures the sustainability of new buildings using metrics like energy use, water conservation, and proximity to public transportation. While useful, the rating system is far from perfect, as it is skewed toward energy efficiency, which is less and less relevant as renewable energy becomes more prevalent. In a sense, the most sustainable building is the one that doesn't get built. That doesn't mean stopping new construction altogether but instead putting focus more on adaptive reuse and upgrading of existing buildings rather than replacing them or building anew.

The **KATHLEEN GRIMM SCHOOL FOR LEADERSHIP AND SUSTAINABILITY AT SANDY GROUND [96]** (or P.S. 62), in Rossville, Staten Island, is a prototype for how future school buildings should be built: It is one of the first net-zero schools in the world, producing the same amount of electricity as it uses per year. This is mainly thanks to 2,023 photovoltaic panels that cover much of its southern facade.

The clever design by SOM brings a lot of natural light to classrooms, thus reducing the need for artificial lighting. The school also has a "bike energy room," where children pedal to generate electricity to power the school. It's a good start, but climate change poses a great danger to a city surrounded by water. The more extreme weather is already here: Record-breaking heat waves, flash floods, and superstorms kill an increasing number of New Yorkers every year. Politicians, on local, state, and federal levels, as well as city planners and private architects need to put more resources and thought into protecting residents by building a more resilient city.

KATHLEEN GRIMM SCHOOL FOR LEADERSHIP AND SUSTAINABILITY AT SANDY GROUND

**KATHLEEN GRIMM SCHOOL FOR
LEADERSHIP AND SUSTAINABILITY
AT SANDY GROUND [96]** *(P.S.62)*
SOM
644 Bloomingdale Rd, Rossville
2015, Staten Island

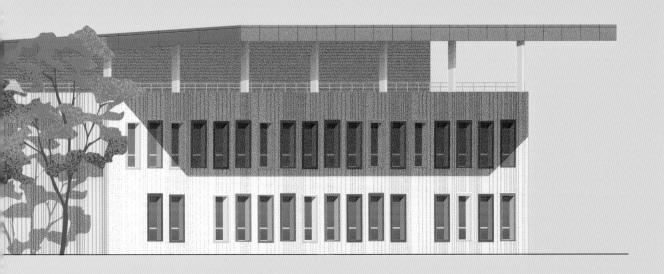

Epilogue

The New York skyline is often portrayed as a poster child of unchecked capitalism, but as we've seen the truth is far more complicated. The skyline is the by-product of a constant struggle between market forces and city regulations (codes, zoning) and incentives (tax breaks). While the scales have always been tipped in big money's favor, city hall has been more than capable of steering the city's own future.

Following Hurricane Sandy, it became obvious that the city needed more than ever to take the lead in adapting to climate change. The increasing frequency of extreme weather and rising sea levels threatens not only property prices, but more importantly the lives of ordinary New Yorkers. Keeping everyone safe, no matter the tax bracket, must be at the forefront of the change. The problem is too complex for a single solution and needs to be sorted out in cooperation between the public and private sectors. It won't be fixed only by switching to electric cars and paper straws.

The city's survival will require solutions from the brightest and the boldest and, luckily, New York City has never had shortage of these types. The city's unique global standing means that other cities around the globe will draw inspiration from trends set there and, consequently, improvement of New York City's climate resilience will have positive repercussions worldwide.

New York City has proven time and again that it can overcome whatever comes its way, be it mass deindustrialization, 9/11, COVID-19, or a worldwide economic meltdown. While climate change may be its biggest challenge yet, it is this author's belief that the city will always prevail.

Endnotes

1 Daniel Okrent, *Great Fortune: The Epic of Rockefeller Center*. (New York: Penguin USA, 2003), 81.

2 Christina Caron, "Macy's Used to Set the Balloons Free, and Other Thanksgiving Day Parade Facts," *The New York Times*, November 20, 2021, https://www.nytimes.com/2021/11/20/nyregion/macys-thanksgiving-parade-facts.html.

3 Graham R. G. *Hodges, Taxi!: A Social History of the New York City Cabdriver*. (New York: NYU Press, 2012), 33.

4 Hodges, *Taxi!*, 48.

5 John Tauranac, *The Empire State Building: The Making of a Landmark*. (New York: St Martin's Press, 1997), 69.

6 Bryn Elliott, "Police Aviation: A History," Pictorial Weekly 4 (1934): 28, http://www.policeaviationnews.com/Acrobat/index/PoliceAviation-ahistory.pdf.

7 Robert A. Caro, *The Power Broker: Robert Moses and the Fall of New York*. (New York: Vintage Books, 1974), 143.

8 Walter Lionel George, *Hail Columbia!: Random Impressions of a Conservative English Radical*. (New York: Harper and Brothers Publishers, 1921), 106.

9 The Editors of New York Magazine, *The Encyclopedia of New York*. (New York: Avid Press Reader, 2020), 322.

10 Tauranac, *The Empire State Building*, 193.

11 Okrent, *Great Fortune*, 294.

12 Andrew J. Sparberg, *From a Nickel to a Token: The Journey from Board of Transportation to MTA*. (New York: Fordham University Press, 2015), 94.

13 Sparberg, *From a Nickel to a Token*, 96-99.

14 Richard Goldstein, *Helluva Town: The Story of New York City During WWII*. (New York: Free Press, 2010), 198.

15 Okrent, *Great Fortune*, 408.

16 Christopher Gray, "A Towering Career; a Collision with War," *The New York Times*, September 6, 2012, https://www.nytimes.com/2012/09/09/realestate/streetscapes-yasuo-matsui-a-career-collides-with-war.html.

17 Aviation Safety Network, "ASN Wikibase Occurrence # 74693," https://aviation-safety.net/wikibase/74693.

18 Kenneth T. Jackson, *WWII & NYC*. (London: Scala Arts Publishers Ltd, 2013), 53.

19 Jackson, *WWII & NYC*, 26.

20 Michael Wilson, "Leaving a Job with a Bus, Not a Slide," The New York Times, August 10, 2010, https://www.nytimes.com/2010/08/11/nyregion/11about.html.

21 Samuel Zipp, *Manhattan Projects: The Rise and Fall of Urban Renewal in Cold War New York*. (New York: Oxford University Press, 2012), 75.

22 The Brownstone Detectives, "When Brooklyn Was (Pre-) Fab (1946)," March 27, 2019, https://www.brownstonedetectives.com/the-brooklyn-housing-shortage-1946/.

23 Robert A.M. Stern, David Fishman, and Thomas Mellins, *New York 1960*. (New York: Monacelli Press, 1995), 342.

24 Michael Snyder and Kurt Soller, "The 25 Most Significant Works of Postwar Architecture," *The New York Times Style Magazine*, August 2, 2021, https://www.nytimes.com/2021/08/02/t-magazine/significant-postwar-architecture.html.

25 The Editors of New York Magazine, *The Encyclopedia of New York*, 322.

26 Hodges, *Taxi!*, 132.

27 Nadine Brozan, "Swimming in the City: Abundance of Pools Makes Cooling Off No Problem," *The New York Times*, July 2, 1976, https://www.nytimes.com/1976/07/02/archives/swimming-in-the-city-abundance-of-pools-makes-cooling-off-no.html.

28 Greg Young, "Toxic Turkey Day: New York City's smoggy holiday crisis," The Bowery Boys, November 11, 2021, https://www.boweryboyshistory.com/2021/11/toxic-turkey-day-new-york-citys-smoggy-holiday-crisis.html.

29 Zipp, *Manhattan Projects*, 21.

30 Nicholas Dagen Bloom and Matthew Gordon Lasner, *Affordable Housing in New York*. (Princeton, NJ: Princeton University Press, 2015), 219-23.

31 Stern, Fishman, and Mellins, *New York 1960*, 928.

32 Paul Goldberger, "Woodhull Hospital, a Controversial Giant, Cast in a 60's Mold; An Appraisal," *The New York Times*, November 5, 1982, https://www.nytimes.com/1982/11/05/nyregion/woodhull-hospital-a-controversial-giant-cast-in-a-60-s-mold-an-appraisal.html.

33 Thomas Dyja, *New York, New York, New York: Four Decades of Success, Excess, and Transformation*. (New York: Simon & Schuster, 2021), 106.

34 Robert A.M. Stern, David Fishman, and Jacob Tilove. *New York 2000*. (New York: Monacelli Press, 2006), 22.

35 Ann Heppermann, interview with Caleb Neelon, David L. Gunn, Vincent DeMarino, and CETE, 99 Percent Invisible, podcast audio, June 3, 2014, https://99percentinvisible.org/episode/clean-trains.

36 Stern, Fishman, and Tilove, *New York 2000*, 71.

37 Ben A. Franklin, "2 Reagan Aides Acted to Speed Portman Hotel," *The New York Times*, December 28, 1981, https://www.nytimes.com/1981/12/28/nyregion/2-reagan-aides-acted-to-speed-portman-hotel.html.

38 Sam Roberts, *America's Mayor: John V. Lindsay and the Reinvention of New York*. (New York: Columbia University Press, 2010), 219.

39 George W. S. Trow, "One Hundred Buildings," *The New Yorker*, October 2, 1970, https://www.newyorker.com/magazine/1970/10/10/one-hundred-buildings.

40 David W. Dunlap, "Building's New Look Shaped by Old Zoning," *The New York Times*, November 14, 1993, https://www.nytimes.com/1993/11/14/realestate/building-s-new-look-shaped-by-old-zoning.html.

41 Pam Belluck, "Neighborhood Report: Long Island City; Group Tells Citibank: Nice Tower, Ugly Sign," *The New York Times*, February 11, 1996, https://www.nytimes.com/1996/02/11/nyregion/neighborhood-report-long-island-city-group-tells-citibank-nice-tower-ugly-sign.html.

42 All That's Interesting, "The Seldom-Heard Story Of New York City's Forgotten Stepchild," ed. Savannah Cox, February 10, 2017, https://allthatsinteresting.com/staten-island-secession.

43 Stern, Fishman, and Tilove, *New York 2000*, 715.

44 Devin Leonard, "The Green Building That's Flunking New York's Climate Law," Bloomberg, March 14, 2022, https://www.bloomberg.com/news/features/2022-03-14/the-green-skyscraper-challenging-nyc-s-emissions-law.

45 Hodges, *Taxi!*, 147-48.

46 Chrofi, "TKTS Times Square," project description, http://www.chrofi.com/project/tkts-times-square, accessed on April 10, 2022.

47 Hodges, *Taxi!*, 161.

48 Daniel Doctoroff, *Greater than Ever: New York's Ultimate Comeback Story*. (New York: Public Affairs Books, 2017), 183.

49 Stern, Fishman, and Tilove, *New York 2000*, 69.

50 Elizabeth Kim, "Did De Blasio Make a Dent in the 'Tale of Two Cities'? A New Analysis of NYC Income Inequality Makes A Case," Gothamist, November 30, 2021, https://gothamist.com/news/did-de-blasio-make-a-dent-in-the-tale-of-two-cities-a-new-analysis-of-nyc-income-equality-makes-a-case.

51 Doctoroff, *Greater than Ever*, 300.

52 Public Surplus, "Auction #2960513 - Staten Island Ferry Iconic JFK double ended passenger & vehicle vessel," auction record, https://www.publicsurplus.com/sms/auction/view?auc=2960513, accessed on February 13, 2022.

Resources and Further Reading

Ballon, Hilary. *Robert Moses and the Modern City: The Transformation of New York*. New York: W. W. Norton & Co., 2008.

Bascomb, Neal. *Higher: A Historic Race to the Sky and the Making of a City*. New York: Doubleday, 2003.

Bloom, Nicholas Dagen and Matthew Gordon Lasner. *Affordable Housing in New York*. Princeton, NJ: Princeton University Press, 2015.

Campanella, Thomas J. *Brooklyn: The Once and Future City*. Princeton, NJ: Princeton University Press, 2019.

Caro, Robert A. *The Power Broke: Robert Moses and the Fall of New York*. New York: Vintage Books, 1974.

Christin, Pierre and Olivier Balez. *Robert Moses: The Master Builder of New York City*. London: Nobrow Press, 2014.

Clausen, Meredith L. *The Pan Am Building*. Cambridge, MA: MIT Press, 2005.

Cohen, Lizabeth. *Saving America's Cities: Ed Logue and the Struggle to Renew Urban America in the Suburban Age*. New York: Farrar, Straus and Giroux, 2019.

Dawson, Ashley. *Extreme Cities: The Peril and Promise of Urban Life in the Age of Climate Change*. Brooklyn: Verso, 2017.

Doctoroff, Daniel. *Greater than Ever: New York's Ultimate Comeback Story*. New York: PublicAffairs Books, 2017.

Dyja, Thomas. *New York, New York, New York*. New York: Simon & Schuster, 2021.

Flamm, Michael W. *In the Heat of the Summer: The New York Riots of 1964 and the War on Crime*. Philadelphia, PA: University of Pennsylvania Press, 2016.

Glanz, James and Eric Lipton. *City in the Sky: The Rise and Fall of the World Trade Center*. New York: Times Books, 2004.

Goldstein, Richard. *Helluva Town: The Story of New York City During WWII*. New York: Free Press, 2010.

Hamill, Pete. *Downtown*. New York: Back Bay Books, 2004.

Jackson, Kenneth T. *The Encyclopedia of New York: Second Edition*. New Haven, CT: Yale University Press, 2011.

Jackson, Kenneth T. *WWII & NYC*. London: Scala Arts Publishers Ltd, 2013.

Jaffe, Steven H. and Jessica Lautin. *Capital of Capital: Money, Banking, and Power in New York City, 1784-2012*. New York: Columbia University Press, 2014.

Koolhaas, Rem. *Delirious New York: A Retroactive Manifesto for Manhattan*. New York: Monacelli Press, 1994.

Mahler, Jonathan. *Ladies and Gentlemen, the Bronx is Burning: 1977, Baseball, Politics, and the Battle for the Soul of a City*. New York: Picador USA, 2006.

Merchants' Association of New York. *Greater New York: Bulletin of the Merchants' Association of New York*. New York: Merchants' Association of New York, 1928.

Moss, Jeremiah. *Vanishing New York: How a Great City Lost Its Soul.* New York: Dey Street Books, 2017.

Nagle, Robin. *Picking Up: On the Streets and Behind the Trucks with the Sanitation Workers of New York City.* New York: Columbia University Press, 2014.

New York Magazine, eds. *The Encyclopedia of New York.* New York: Avid Reader Press, 2020.

Okrent, Daniel. *Great Fortune: The Epic of Rockefeller Center.* New York: Penguin USA, 2003.

Phillips-Fein, Kim. *Fear City: New York's Fiscal Crisis and the Rise of Austerity Politics.* New York: Metropolitan Books, 2017.

Raab, Selwyn. *Five Families: The Rise, Decline, and Resurgence of America's Most Powerful Mafia Empires.* New York: Griffin, 2006.

Roberts, Sam. *America's Mayor: John V. Lindsay and the Reinvention of New York.* New York: Columbia University Press, 2010.

Robins, Anthony W. *New York Art Deco: A Guide to Gotham's Jazz Age Architecture.* New York: Excelsior Editions, 2017.

Russell, Graham and Gao Hodges. *Taxi!: A Social History of the New York City Cabdriver.* New York: NYU Press, 2012.

Sasek, Miroslav. *This Is New York.* New York: Universe Publishing, 1960.

Soffer, Jonathan M. *Ed Koch and the Rebuilding of New York City.* New York: Columbia University Press, 2012.

Sorkin, Michael. *What Goes Up: The Right and Wrongs to the City.* New York: Verso, 2018.

Sparberg, Andrew J. *From a Nickel to a Token: The Journey from Board of Transportation to MTA.* New York: Fordham University Press, 2015.

Stern, Robert A.M., Gregory Gilmartin, and Thomas Mellins. *New York 1930.* New York: Rizzoli International Publications, 1987.

Stern, Robert A.M., Thomas Mellins, and David Fishman. *New York 1960.* New York: Monacelli Press, 1995.

Stern, Robert A.M., David Fishman, and Jacob Tilove. *New York 2000.* New York: Monacelli Press, 2006.

Tauranac, John. *The Empire State Building: The Making of a Landmark.* New York: St Martin's Press, 1997.

Trager, James. *The New York Chronology.* New York: HarperCollins, 2003.

Wertz, Julia. *Tenements, Towers & Trash: An Unconventional Illustrated History of New York City.* New York: Black Dog & Leventhal Publishers Inc., 2017.

White, Norval, Elliot Willensky, and Fran Leadon. *AIA Guide to New York City: Fifth Edition.* New York: Oxford University Press, 2010.

Young, Greg and Tom Meyers. *The Bowery Boys: Adventures in Old New York.* New York: Ulysses Press, 2016.

Zipp, Samuel. *Manhattan Projects.* New York: Oxford University Press, 2012.

Further Watching

Documentaries

The Police Tapes, directed by Alan Raymond and Susan Raymond, 1977

New York: A Documentary Film, directed by Ric Burns, 1999

Man on Wire, directed by James Marsh, 2008

The Central Park Five, directed by Ken Burns, Sarah Burns, and David McMahon, 2012

NY77: The Coolest Year in Hell, directed by Henry Corra, 2007

Everybody Street, directed by Cheryl Dunn, 2013

Citizen Jane: Battle for the City, directed by Matt Tyrnauer, 2016

A Night at the Garden, directed by Marshall Curry, 2017

The Booksellers, directed by D.W. Young, 2019

The Price of Everything, directed by Nathaniel Kahn, 2018

Breslin and Hamill: Deadline Artists, directed by Jonathan Alter, John Block, and Steve McCarthy, 2018

Films

King Kong, directed by Merian C. Cooper & Ernest B. Schoedsack, 1933

The House on 92nd Street, directed by Henry Hathaway, 1945

The Naked City, directed by Jules Dassin, 1948

The Killer that Stalked New York, directed by Earl McEvoy, 1951

Little Fugitive, directed by Ray Ashley, Morris Engel, and Ruth Orkin, 1953

On the Waterfront, directed by Elia Kazan, 1954

On the Bowery, directed by Lionel Rogosin, 1956

Sweet Smell of Success, directed by Alexander Mackendrick, 1957

The Apartment, directed by Billy Wilder, 1960

West Side Story, directed by Jerome Robbins and Robert Wise, 1961

Blast of Silence, directed by Allen Baron, 1961

The Out-of-Towners, directed by Arthur Hiller, 1970

Shaft, directed by Gordon Parks, 1971

The French Connection, directed by William Friedkin, 1971

Serpico, directed by Sidney Lumet, 1973

The Taking of Pelham One Two Three, directed by Joseph Sargent, 1974

Taxi Driver, directed by Martin Scorsese, 1976

Saturday Night Fever, directed
by John Badham, 1977

Eyes of Laura Mars, directed
by Irvin Kershner, 1978

Wolfen, directed by Michael Wadleigh, 1981

Escape from New York, directed
by John Carpenter, 1981

The Muppets Take Manhattan,
directed by Frank Oz, 1984

After Hours, directed by Martin Scorsese, 1985

Wall Street, directed by Oliver Stone, 1985

Working Girl, directed by Mike Nichols, 1988

Coming to America, directed
by John Landis, 1988

Do the Right Thing, directed by Spike Lee, 1989

Bonfire of the Vanities, directed
by Brian De Palma, 1990

State of Grace, directed by Phil Joanou
and Michael Lee Baron, 1990

Kids, directed by Larry Clark, 1995

Godzilla, directed by Roland Emmerich, 1998

Summer of Sam, directed by Spike Lee, 1999

Bringing Out the Dead, directed
by Martin Scorsese, 1999

American Psycho, directed by Mary Harron, 2000

Requiem for a Dream, directed
by Darren Aronofsky, 2000

Spider-Man, directed by Sam Raimi, 2002

25th Hour, directed by Spike Lee, 2003

King Kong, directed by Peter Jackson, 2005

The Wolf of Wall Street, directed
by Martin Scorsese, 2013

The Big Short, directed by Adam McKay, 2015

If Beale Street Could Talk, directed
by Barry Jenkins, 2018

Spider-Man: Into the Spider-Verse,
directed by Bob Persichetti, Peter
Ramsey, and Rodney Rothman, 2018

Motherless Brooklyn, directed
by Edward Norton, 2019

Uncut Gems, directed by Benny
Safdie and Josh Safdie, 2019

The King of Staten Island, directed
by Judd Apatow, 2020

An American Pickle, directed
by Brandon Trost, 2020

Acknowledgments

This book is dedicated to Lilly, who provided me with the inspiration, the energy, and the brains for those long four years I spent working on it. She also made this book look beautiful. I love you.

Massive thanks to my editor, Ron Broadhurst, for all his guidance, patience, and wisdom. Also cheers to Lynn Scrabis for bringing it together and to Lillian Dondero and Elizabeth Fazzare for all the tough editing and great suggestions. Thanks, also, to the amazingly helpful John Kriskiewicz for his support and connections. My gratitude also goes to wonderful writer David Sokol for his suggestions and for connecting me with Rizzoli. Thanks to the brilliant Nina Cosford for her wordsmith skills, the great Charlotte Godhart for her suggestions, and the superb Faride Mereb for amazing design tips.

I can't forget about Milan Moffatt and Phil Chmalts: thank you for lending us your Brooklyn pad! Also, a very belated thank you to my friend Tallulah Morris for her help with the draft of my first book, *Modern London*. And related to that, thanks to superwoman Sue Henriot for successfully unloading dozens of copies of the book onto her friends.

And last, but not least, a massive thank you to my mum, Vendina, and sisters, Vivi and Marcelik. I wouldn't have been able to do any of this without you.

About the Author

Lukas Novotny is an author, illustrator, and graphic designer. Originally from the Czech Republic, he studied architecture and civil engineering before settling in London. His first book, *Modern London: An Illustrated Cityscape from the 1920s to the Present Day*, was shortlisted for the British Book Design Awards 2019.

Illustrations in this book are available as prints on his website at www.lukasnovo.com.

Modern New York

First published in the United States of America in 2023 by
Rizzoli International Publications, Inc.
300 Park Avenue South
New York, NY 10010
www.rizzoliusa.com

Publisher: Charles Miers
Editor: Ron Broadhurst
Design: Lilly Marques
Production Manager: Colin Hough-Trapp
Managing Editor: Lynn Scrabis

This book was typeset in Name Sans, Stephen Nixon
of Arrow Type. This is a modern interpretation of the tile
mosaic name tablets of the New York City subway.

Printed in Hong Kong

2023 2024 2025 2026 / 10 9 8 7 6 5 4 3 2 1

ISBN: 978-0-8478-9949-4

Library of Congress Control Number: 2023904935

Visit us online:
Facebook.com/RizzoliNewYork
Twitter: @Rizzoli_Books
Instagram.com/RizzoliBooks
Pinterest.com/RizzoliBooks
Youtube.com/user/RizzoliNY
Issuu.com/Rizzoli